*Poems by Two Brothers*

Elizabeth Russell, née Tennyson (1776-1865), Muse of the Two Brothers.
Pastel by John Russell, 1805 (Tennyson Research Centre Collection).

# POEMS BY TWO BROTHERS:

*The Lives, Work and Influence of*
*George Clayton Tennyson*
*and*
*Charles Tennyson d'Eyncourt*

Christopher Sturman and Valerie Purton

'Look here upon this picture, and on this,
The counterfeit presentment of two brothers.'
(*Hamlet*, III, iv)

PAUL WATKINS
STAMFORD
1993

© 1993 Christopher Sturman and Valerie Purton

Published by
PAUL WATKINS
18, Adelaide Street, Stamford, Lincolnshire, PE9 2EN.

ISBN
1 871615 38 0

Photoset from the discs of the authors by the publisher

*Printed on long-life paper*

Printed and bound by Woolnough's of Irthlingborough.

*For*
Mary E. Sturman
*and in memory of*
John H. Sturman
*and of*
Dinah Anderson

# CONTENTS

# PREFACE

In 1827 J. & J. Jackson of Louth printed Alfred Tennyson's first collection of poems. Entitled *Poems by Two Brothers*, it contained in fact poems from the three eldest Tennysons, Alfred, Charles and Frederick. The title suggests the importance of family ties to the poet in his early years. In the following pages we hope to trace the Tennysons' love of poetry back into the previous generation by bringing together for the first time the work of an earlier pair of brothers, the poet's father George Clayton Tennyson (1778-1831) and his uncle, Charles Tennyson d'Eyncourt (1784-1861). The two brothers' relationship with *their* father, the redoubtable George Tennyson ('The Old Man of the Wolds' as he was known to his Somersby grandchildren), who by tradition 'disinherited' the elder in favour of the younger son, was, says the poet's biographer Robert Bernard Martin, 'probably the main external fact governing the life of his grandson Alfred'.

Alfred's relationship with his Uncle Charles is complex. The Somersby children overtly despised their uncle for his conventionality; perhaps secretly and more seriously, they envied, on their father's behalf, his worldly success (Charles became M.P. for Grimsby when Alfred was only nine). Besides this, in a household increasingly damaged by drunkenness and violence, the Doctor's gentler sons, Charles and Alfred, deflected blame from their father (as is evident in *Poems by Two Brothers*) and focused their resentment on the figure of their uncle. Here was an adult with considerable power, who was not vulnerable, not a victim: he rather than his brother was to bear the brunt of his nephews' adolescent rebellion.

George Clayton Tennyson's personality has long been acknowledged as having had a powerful impact on that of his impressionable third son. Fear of epilepsy, melancholia and a sense of being doomed to share the 'black blood' of the Tennysons, were all part of Alfred's inheritance. Between the ages of eleven and eighteen he lived with a deeply-troubled personality who was not only his father but also his spiritual mentor and only teacher. He was torn between deep affection and pity for the father he saw as victim and hatred and aggression towards the uncle and grandfather he saw as all-powerful and malevolent. The effect of such intense exposure to a parent (reminiscent of the well-documented examples of the Mill and the Gosse families) is evident not only in Alfred's early poetry but perhaps also in the poet's life-long search for consolation, suggested perhaps in the 'secure' abba form of the *In Memoriam* stanzas where doubt is shaped and ultimately controlled. In his greatest work, in "Ulysses" and "Tithonus" particularly, the central figure is old, hungry, unfulfilled; only in *Maud* is the unhappy life of a father remodelled by a son who finally escapes his example.

It is now fifty years since W. D. Paden's *Tennyson in Egypt: A Study of the Imagery in His Earlier Work* was first published, and since then scholars have followed this pioneering essay, charting the richness of the library at Somersby as an influence on the young Alfred. The link between Alfred's poetic development and his father's poetry, however, has never been thoroughly examined. The poems were part of his childhood and adolescence. Their imagery and the poetic parameters they set up helped form Alfred's own poetic world and set out its early limits and concerns, not only in *Poems by Two Brothers* but later in his career.

Throughout, our aim has been, so far as it is possible, to let the main characters speak for themselves in their letters and poems; to this end our main debt is owed to the staff of the Lincolnshire Archives Office, and especially Nigel Colley, Peter Noon and Ged Payne who over the years have provided us with hundreds of bundles of Tennyson d'Eyncourt family papers for inspection. Sue Gates of the Tennyson Research Centre has been ever helpful in making George Clayton Tennyson's Commonplace Book available for study; Robert Woof of the Wordsworth Trust and Gemma Hunter of Orleans House Gallery have kindly given us access during the months of this centenary year when it was removed from Lincoln. Edgar F. Shannon Jr, Norman Page and Roger Evans have given unfailing encouragement. Jim Murray of Tealby has been particularly generous in sharing with us his encylopaedic knowledge of the Tennyson d'Eyncourt archive. We also acknowledge the debt we owe to two biographers: to the late Sir Charles Tennyson for his pioneering research on his grandfather; and to Robert Bernard Martin (whose *Tennyson: The Unquiet Heart* is itself the product of full immersion in the Tennyson d'Eyncourt papers) for many insights and for providing some of the numerous parallels we see with *Hamlet*. Finally we are indebted to Chrisopher Ricks, whose magisterial edition, *The Poems of Tennyson*, has been our constant companion, and a model for our, inevitably modest, *Poems by Two Brothers*.

We are grateful to the following for permission to reproduce copyright material: Lincolnshire County Council and Lord Tennyson (Tennyson Research Centre Collection); Lincolnshire County Council Recreational Services (Local Studies Collection, Lincoln Central Library); Mr M. A. E. Tennyson d'Eyncourt and Lincolnshire Archives; Lord Cobbold and the Hertfordshire Record Office; and The Beinecke Rare Book and Manuscript Library, Yale University.

Finally, we would like to thank proof-reader Philip Riley and publisher Shaun Tyas for coping with the double difficulty of working with two authors.

Christopher Sturman and Valerie Purton
November 1992

# LIST OF ILLUSTRATIONS

# ABBREVIATIONS

| | |
|---|---|
| 'Alfred's father' | [Sir] Charles Tennyson, 'Tennyson papers. I. Alfred's father', *Cornhill Magazine*, 153 (March 1935), pp. 283-305. |
| Colvin | Howard Colvin, *A Biographical Dictionary of British Architects 1600-1840* (London, 1978). |
| H.R.O. | Hertfordshire Record Office, Hertford. |
| L.A.O. | Lincolnshire Archives Office, Lincoln. |
| *Letters A.T.* | Cecil Y. Lang and Edgar F. Shannon, Jr, eds, *The Letters of Alfred Lord Tennyson*, 3 vols (Oxford, 1981-1990). |
| Martin | Robert Bernard Martin, *Tennyson: The Unquiet Heart* (London and Oxford, 1980). |
| *Memoir* | [Hallam Tennyson], *Alfred Lord Tennyson: A Memoir by his Son*, 2 vols (London, 1897). |
| Paden | W. D. Paden, *Tennyson in Egypt: A Study of the Imagery in His Earlier Work* (Lawrence, Kansas, 1942). |
| *Poems A.T.* | Christopher Ricks, ed., *The Poems of Tennyson*, 2nd edn, 3 vols (Harlow, 1987). |
| T.R.C. | Tennyson Research Centre, Lincoln. |
| *T.R.B.* | *Tennyson Research Bulletin.* |
| Tennyson & Dyson | Sir Charles Tennyson and Hope Dyson, *The Tennysons: Background to Genius* (London, 1974). |

In the transcription of manuscript letters, the original spellings have been retained; most abbreviations have been expanded; the writers' (often highly inconsistent) use of capital letters has been brought into line with modern use; some slight changes have been made to the punctuation (though within sentences, original punctuation has largely been retained). Where the dates of letters are not indicated in the text, they are given in the foot-notes. Any material supplied is within square brackets.

The same principle governs the transcription of the manuscript poems, but the ampersand (&), which we have retained in the letters, has been replaced by *and*.

The texts of Alfred's poetry reproduce the first printed versions; only for *Maud* (1855) has a later edition been used, in this case the (enlarged) second edition of 1856.

# TWO BROTHERS

George Tennyson (1750-1835), Alfred, Lord Tennyson's grandfather, married Mary Turner (1753-1825), daughter of John Turner, Esquire, of Caistor, in June 1776. He was ambitious, determined, even hard in pursuit of a successful career as a solicitor; she was mild, loving, religious and artistic. Their marriage seems to have been reasonably happy, though their success as parents is much more doubtful. Their four children were brought up very differently from each other, and it is probably here that one must look for the source of many of the future tensions in the family.[1]

The two daughters, Elizabeth (born 1776) and Mary (born 1777), were quite unlike in character. Mary was sent to stay with her mother's parents, the Turners, until she was eleven. Her adult life when married to John Bourne of Dalby was marked by gloominess and an adherence to Calvinist views, memorably recorded by her nephew: 'Alfred, Alfred, when I look at you, I think of the words of Holy Scripture - "Depart from me, ye cursed, into everlasting fire."'[2] Elizabeth was kept at home and, by all accounts, became her parents' darling. She was vivacious, funny and deeply attached to both her brothers, who remained influenced by her all their lives.

George (born 1778) seems from the beginning to have been an awkward and moody child. Like Mary he was sent off to grandparents to be brought up, in his case to his paternal grandfather, Michael Tennyson (1721-1796), an apothecary at Hedon in Holderness. Probably overindulged as a small child, he never settled well on his return to his parents' home: Mary Tennyson reported to her mother in 1785, 'our house is all noise and distraction since George and his grandfather came, I think I never saw a child so rude and ungovernable as he is'.[3] His relationship with his father was always marked by friction, though the elder George, contrary to popular legend, did in fact make careful provision for his son at every stage of his life. As early as 1791 (when George was only thirteen) his father secured from Mr Heneage 'the living of South Willingham and another in that neighbourhood [?Benniworth]'[4]

---

1    For general family background see [Sir] Charles Tennyson, *Alfred Tennyson* (London, 1949); Sir Charles Tennyson and Hope Dyson, *The Tennysons: Background to Genius* (London, 1974); and Robert Bernard Martin, *Tennyson: The Unquiet Heart* (London and Oxford, 1980). These important studies have established what is by now a reasonably well known story; in order to reduce the number of footnotes, no references have been given to them unless they furnish either a significant point of detail or a quotation. For useful descriptions of the Tennyson d'Eyncourt deposit at L.A.O., providing additional biographical information, see Lincolnshire Archives Committee *Archivists' Report*, [2] (1950-51), pp.5-8; 8 (1956-57), pp.8-11; 10 (1958-59), pp.28-30; 12 (1960-61), pp.44-45; 14 (1962-63), pp.28-31; 16 (1964-65), pp.21-23; also 12 (1960-61), pp.41-44 (Tennyson deposit).

2    *Memoir*, I, p.15.

3    L.A.O. Tenn. 2/7/23, 17 May 1785. Mary Tennyson, preparing to visit Sixhills, wrote again to her mother on 30 May : 'I leave George and his father and grandfather to keep house if they can but agree' (Tenn. 2/7/24).

4    T.R.C. Letter 2437B, W. Hutton to George Tennyson, 20 January 1791.

with an eye to his son's future incumbency. Unsuited though he undoubtedly was to much of the work involved in the life of a clergyman, George showed little aptitude later in life for any other career (except that of penniless scholar). It is perhaps too easy to criticise Old George for what might well have been a wise move on behalf of his son.

It was obvious from their early years that George's younger brother Charles (born 1784) was much more suited to establishing the family socially. Charles shared his brother's dark good looks, but enjoyed an equable temperament. His life, in contrast to George's, was marked by reasonable worldly success and outward calm. Dr Orme, headmaster of Louth School, wrote of him in 1798, 'His disposition is so amiable, that it will probably procure general esteem from mankind as he goes out into the world.'[1] It is not surprising therefore that he basked all his life in the approval and favour of his father. (Only his liberal opinions on matters like the Reform Bill and Catholic Emancipation proved too much for the rest of his family - including, it must be said, the young Alfred, much more conservative politically even in his youth.)

Young George was sent at the age of eleven to the free Grammar School in York. A significant insight into his early poetic talent is offered in the diary of Lewis Carroll for 2 January 1861: recording a visit to Christ Church by Canon Gray of Ripon he noted, 'He also mentioned that he was at school with Dr. Tennyson (father of the poet), and was a great favourite of his. He remembers that Tennyson used to do his school-translations in rhyme.'[2] He was then boarded with Mr Hutchinson of Holywell in Huntingdonshire to be prepared for Cambridge. In 1796 he went up to St John's College. At first, Charles's schooldays followed a similar pattern. His parents had moved from Market Rasen to Lincoln in c.1791 and to begin with he too was sent to York, but in c.1794 was removed to Lincoln School. When the family moved to Grimsby in 1798, he was transferred to the grammar school at Louth; in 1801 he followed his brother to St John's.

In February 1795, when he was twelve years old, Charles was chosen to read the Introductory Address at Lincoln School's Speech Day, and achieved the distinction of being mentioned in *The Gentleman's Magazine*.[3] The dignified but predictable iambic pentameters, probably written by the school's headmaster, the Revd John Carter, obviously influenced Charles's own taste. Though liberal in politics he was unwaveringly conservative in literary matters (as his unfailingly negative response to Alfred's poetry shows). His own *Eustace; an Elegy* (London, 1851) suggests a conventional talent unable to grow beyond its earliest influences. The lines from that speech day could fit seamlessly into *Eustace*:

[1]   T.R.C. Letter 4603, 15 December 1798.
[2]   Stuart Dodgson Collingwood, *The Life and Letters of Lewis Carroll...* (London, 1898), p.80; also Roger Lancelyn Green (ed.), *The Diaries of Lewis Carroll*, 2 vols (London, 1954), I, p.165. Canon Gray (the diary gives the spelling as Grey) was the second son of Old George's friend William Gray, attorney of York.
[3]   *Gentleman's Magazine* (March 1795), 240; Charles Garton, 'Lincoln School speech day, 1795: a Tennyson connection?', *T.R.B.*, 5, 5 (1991), pp. 248-59.

Such is that study, such the moral plan,
Which moulds the boy, and forms the future man.
Nor shall the infant Muse's humble lay
The debt of gratitude forget to pay
To those preceptors whose impressive rule
Sway'd through revolving years this ancient school....

Despite or perhaps because of their contrasting temperaments, the brothers enjoyed a friendship which bridged the six years' difference in their ages and was cemented by their shared passion for literature. In their teens they collaborated on several dramatic works, the most complete of which are "The Tragedy of Gonzalo and Delia" and the "Castle of Otranto".[1] The theme was a popular one: Horace Walpole's Gothic novel *The Castle of Otranto* (1764) was still very much in vogue at the end of the century.

The dedications in the manuscript of the plays suggest already the characters of the brothers. The first, in Charles's bold, youthful hand, is to Miss Anne Fellowes.[2] It suggests a boy confident of his powers to charm (Charles was to be all his life almost dangerously successful with women); it shows a real love of literature but little originality; and it bears already Charles's characteristic tone of disarming complacency:

Madam,
I take the liberty of inscribing this little book to your perusal, as I know you possess all the endowments & abilities of the mind combined with virtue & elegance. Bound even with the chains of goodness resting upon the anchor of hope. What honour can extend the bonds of virtue? This book contains the nature of man which is the gift of your most obedient humble servant & well-wisher

Charles Tennyson

The manuscript contains another dedication, in the cramped, introspective hand of George. He does not go outside the family for his Muse, choosing his beloved sister 'Miss Eliza Tennyson':

Madam,
Your condescending character makes me presume to put my Otranto under your protection. If you vouchsafe to accept it I cannot doubt of its reception amongst the English ladies. The vertues of Isabella cannot fail to recommend it to you if the obscurity of the author doth not make you disdain to read her story. I would not presume to bring your excellent character within the narrow compass of a dedication; you will find it drawn at large, through the whole play, in that of Isabella.

[1] L.A.O. T.d'E. H156.
[2] Anne Fellowes was the daughter of Dr William Fellowes who practised in Lincoln during the 1790s. He is listed as a tenant of the Priory in 1790 and in 1796 (L.A.O. LL 3/13 & 4/13) and would therefore have been a near neighbour of the Tennysons who lived in Deloraine Court; Elizabeth Tennyson wrote to her grandmother, Mrs Turner, on 17 September 1797, 'We have not yet heard what physician takes Dr. Fellowes's house....' (L.A.O. Tenn. 2/1/31).

That you may live long the patroness of vertue and that you may be bless'd
with all that can make your state happy is the hearty wish of Madam

Your most devoted
Most obedient
Most humble Servant
George Clayton Tennyson

Beneath the same conventional flourishes here is the stress on diffidence and
unworthiness. 'I would not presume' suggests the Prayer of Humble Access in the
Communion Service. The child is father to the man: here Charles is direct and bold,
George periphrastic and uncertain - and this is how they were each to remain. The
poses adopted in their portraits, painted in the 1810s, once more uncannily
emphasise this contrast (Figs 1 and 2).

As they grew up it must have become increasingly obvious to the two boys
that their own sibling roles were strangely reversed. George's play, 'my Otranto',
with the usurpation by Manfredi at its centre, deals with displacement and loss of
rightful possessions. It is possibly in Charles's hand, but, being so much the younger,
he was probably the amanuensis. The tone is very much George's:

O conscience, conscience, terrible avenger
Why dartest thou thy pois'nous stings so deep
Refusing comfort to my tortur'd mind?
Me miserable! which way shall I fly
How shall I 'scape the goads of keen remorse?

George's later poem, "The Wandering Jew", strikes a similar note; the restless guilty
outcast was obviously a figure he found particularly congenial. The blank verse too
suggests George: his younger brother was only ever at home in rhyming couplets.
This partnership in verse, however incomplete, is a touching indication of the
closeness of the family, despite the truculence of both the older and the younger
George.

George's years at Cambridge were a continuing time of unease for his father,
who went so far as to have the boy's former tutor Mr Hutchinson check up on his
activities. Nothing was found amiss in the young man's conduct, however. He duly
obtained a pass degree and on 11 May 1801 was ordained deacon. The gravitation of
an eccentric, scholarly young man into the Church in the early nineteenth century
should not occasion surprise among twentieth-century literary historians; it was a
profession which suited many aspects of George's character. He was, as the contents
of his library attest, deeply interested in theological studies, possessing many editions
of the Old and New Testaments as well as Hebrew and Syriac grammar books.
Somersby tradition has it, however, that at about this time George was openly
disinherited by his father, with the implication that he was forced against his will
into the Church. Hallam Tennyson records the reaction of Mr Heneage, to the elder
George: 'George, if you do this you'll certainly be damned, you will indeed.'[1]

---

[1]  *Memoir*, I, p.13.

Figure 1: George Clayton Tennyson (1778-1831). Oil possibly by John Harrison (Tennyson Research Centre Collection).

Figure 2: Charles Tennyson, later Tennyson d'Eyncourt (1784-1861).
Oil by John Harrison, *c.*1810 (Tennyson Research Centre Collection).

TWO BROTHERS

Before taking up his duties, and possibly as a reward for his compliance (though it might equally well have been to get him out of the way), George was able, presumably at his father's expense, to visit Russia in the autumn of 1801, for the coronation of the new Tzar, Alexander. All manner of fantastical stories cluster in family tradition around this visit - all suggesting a character of Peer Gynt-like uncertainty, trying to establish a sense of identity. There are stories of George narrowly escaping with his life from the court at St Petersburg, of his flight into the Crimea, his illness in a peasant's hut, and his eventual escape by answering the horn call of an English courier.[1] What is certain is that he returned in very poor health in February 1802, was ordained priest on 19 December of that year and was inducted two days later as rector of Benniworth near Louth.

Over the years the elder George sedulously consolidated the family's economic and social position through the purchase of land, notably the manor of Beacons at Tealby. In 1797 his daughter Elizabeth wrote to her grandmother Turner:

> You will be surprised to hear that my father has sold his house to Mr. Burton for £1500 & we quit next May day. We shall be at Grimsby for some time.... My father thinks of building a house from the old foundations at Tealby. We none of us regret quitting Lincoln - every body agreeable seems tired of the place & talk of leaving.... [W]e must own that the generality of Lincoln people are not pleasant.[2]

Old George commissioned plans from the Hull architect George Pycock for a new house at Tealby,[3] though it was not until 1801 that he moved there. The house was at first called Tealby Lodge; only from c.1811 was it referred to as Bayons Manor.

When in 1805, young George married Elizabeth Fytche, the gentle daughter of a former vicar of Louth and niece of the Bishop of Lincoln, he cannot have displeased his father, though he was later to speak of himself as being, in the eyes of his aspiring family, simply a 'poor parson'. At the end of December 1806 he was presented by Mr Burton to the rectories of Somersby and Bag Enderby. A letter to his father of July 1807 describing the building work at Somersby is typical, in its worrying over finances, of many sent over the years:

> My dear Father
> You were so good as to say that you would contribute £200 towards the building of the house at Somersby. All the materials for the house and stables have been procured and the house partly finished. The man with whom I have contracted has applied to me for money for the payment of the labourers and the materials & states that being poor he will otherwise lose his credit & cannot proceed. I cannot answer his demand which now amounts to more than £100 as

1   *Memoir*, II, pp.147-48; Patrick Waddington, *Tennyson and Russia* (Lincoln, 1987), pp.1-4.
2   L.A.O. Tenn. 2/1/31, 17 September 1797. Old George had bought Deloraine Court for £600 in 1794 (L.A.O. 2T.d'E. H94/2 ; also 2T.d'E. H94, an inventory of the contents of the house). He had inherited in 1794 substantial interests in Grimsby under the will of his uncle, Christopher Clayton. For his economic and political interests there, see Gordon Jackson, *Grimsby and the Haven Company 1796-1846* (Grimsby, 1971) and Edward Gillett, *A History of Grimsby* (Oxford, 1970), *passim*.
3   L.A.O. T.d'E. H169/1-2.

the house at Benniworth has taken away all my ready money. Will you give me leave to draw upon your account at Lincoln bank? Mr. Burton promised to give me £50 but so far from receiving that I been have not yet got the half yearly income of the livings which has been due since the 12th of May. The house was in so miserable a state that I have been obliged to take down the ceilings of the whole house above & below, except of two rooms. This together with the enlarging of the kitchen which was only ten feet wide, the building of a nursery over it & two servants' rooms above the nursery without which I should not have had room even for my own family (not taking into consideration the variety of places there are to build besides, such as coal house &c as there were no accomodations [sic] of this kind anywhere) will cost more than the 120£ which I suppose would have covered the expence. Mr. Burton gave both you & my self a false idea of the house. To make it at all decent it will cost at least itself £200 & Mr. Burton should give me another £50 if he does not wish me to be much out of pocket. Had I indeed known all the disagreeable circumstances connected with the livings I never could have been induced to accept them. Mr. Burton in his two last letters has been desirous that I should raise the tithe of his brother's & Mrs. Buckworth's tenants & says this must be done by the rector tho' for my benefit. Thus, with no advantage to myself at my first entrance into residence am I to incur an odium; abstracted from the consideration of it being perhaps a simoniacal payment to raise the tithes of a living & give all the advantage to the patron without any further composition. I should before this have come over to Tealby but I have no horse & walking is but disagreeable this hot weather. Eliza unites with me in best affection to all & believe me my dear Father

Your's affectionately<br>
G.C. Tennyson[1]

George and Eliza with their young son Frederick (born 1807) moved into the Rectory before the birth of their second son, Charles, in the summer of 1808; Alfred, their third son, was born there in August of the following year.

When Charles graduated from Cambridge in 1805, he began his pupillage (he had been admitted to the Inner Temple in 1801); he was called to the Bar in November 1806 and moved to chambers in Boswell Court. Whilst in London, in May 1807, he met the heiress Frances ('Fanny') Hutton (1787-1878) of Morton near Gainsborough. After a lengthy and difficult courtship, during which his father investigated Fanny's background and argued about the settlement, the couple were married at Gainsborough on New Year's Day 1808. Charles's health soon began to give cause for concern. He consulted medical men in Lincolnshire (Dr Barton of Market Rasen and Dr Harrison of Horncastle) as well as Dr Baillie in London, who, he advised his father on 16 March 1808, 'thinks all my complaints arise from a bad digestion and consequent continual clogs in my stomach and bowels....'[2] Within a few days Charles had a fit. 'Poor Fanny was so terrified', he informed Old George, 'She has been in a terror ever since. She had indeed much reason for I believe I was within two minutes of death - Baillie said it would have been over with me if I had

1    L.A.O. T.d'E. H144/57, 24 July 1807.
2    L.A.O. T.d'E. H65/4, 16 March 1808.

not turned sick the convulsion at my stomach relaxing.'[1] Following a further consultation he reassured his father once more:

> [Baillie] retains his first inclination that my disease arises from a bad secretion of bile & a foul state of stomach and bowels. The alternative would be a mild species of epilepsy yet with no decided character. I am to pursue calomel with Epsom Salts mixed with a tonic to remove the supposed cause and to continue abstinence from wine to provide against what we all trust my complaint is not - since that would promote and assist any determination of blood to the head....[2]

Charles recovered from this attack, but his letters, as much as those written later by his brother, show that he was morbidly preoccupied with his own health. His mother, writing in January 1809, saw the situation clearly:

> Tell us the worst because suspense is less bearable. Have you had a direct attack of your complaint or only symptoms? and what are the symptoms? for you cannot for a moment doubt your father's or my own acquiescence to any plan recommended by Dr. Harrison for your ultimate benefit. You deplore the irritable state of your nerves - as having an effect upon your temper. I really wish you believe it originates in your disease but don't let this or any thing else prey upon your spirits - for the health of the body will fall as a sacrafice [sic] to the mind if too much indulged....[3]

For the rest of his life Charles was periodically unwell with symptoms which do suggest epilepsy, an illness which ultimately was to affect seriously the life of his brother, as well as manifesting itself in the next generation of Tennysons.[4]

———

George was a man of great charm and culture: his 'social powers were famous throughout the countryside',[5] he played the harp and over the years assembled a large library whose contents reflect his catholic taste.[6] During the early years of his

1   L.A.O. T.d'E. H65/8, [22] March 1808.
2   L.A.O. T.d'E. H65/9, 25 March 1808.
3   L.A.O. T.d'E. H149/4, 14 January 1809. On 1 February 1809, Charles supplied his father with a copy of his letter to Mr Chaplin of Blankney declining the offer of a captaincy in the Militia: 'My health for some time past has been very much disordered and the physicians have uniformly enjoined me to abstain from much walking exercise and avoid wet feet; by availing myself of your very obliging offer I fear I should frequently expose myself to a breach of the injunction in both points, and the consequences, I am taught to apprehend, would be too serious for me of indulging my inclination by becoming a Captain in your Regiment....' (L.A.O. T.d'E. H67/2).
4   Charles's eldest son, George Hildeyard (1809-1871) certainly was epileptic (below, p. 12) and never married. For George Clayton Tennyson's family see in particular Ann C. Colley, *Tennyson and Madness* (Athens, Georgia, 1983), esp. pp.34-50. Old George may also have been a sufferer from epilepsy, and the strain of 'madness' can be traced back to his Clayton forebears - see Tennyson & Dyson, pp.17-19.
5   *Memoir*, I, p.16.
6   The 'Inventory and Valuation of the Furniture, Plate, Linen, Books, and other effects of the late Dr. Tennyson...' (T.R.C.), drawn up for probate in June 1831, is especially useful. Nancie Campbell, *Tennyson in Lincoln* I (Lincoln, 1971), pp.1-23, lists Dr Tennyson's books at T.R.C.

marriage he worked on various literary projects. His Commonplace Book,[1] commenced in 1807, with an appropriate mock half-title and title page (Fig. 3) reveals the extent of his interests. Among the substantial contributions are detailed (and illustrated) directions on book-binding (George recorded that the volume was 'Bound by me / March 1807'), an account 'Painting in Oil' with lists of the painters of various schools, and 'An essay in vindication of the divine benevolence' - here again George set out a title page (now badly torn) with an epigraph from Milton and the (intended) printer '[... J]ackson, Market Place, Louth'. There are various household accounts, a listing of the parishioners of Somersby and Bag Enderby for 1807/8 and numerous drawings and sketches. George also recorded here a number of his poems (manuscripts of additional works survive amongst the Tennyson d'Eyncourt family papers). The earliest is perhaps "A Sublime Ode in Two Parts on Wintry Weather" which can be dated to c.1806. His sister Elizabeth, who in 1798 had married the wealthy Matthew Russell of Hardwicke House, Co. Durham, was, once more, his Muse. Her return to Hardwicke, following a visit to Lincolnshire, is commemorated in the "Verses Addressed to a Lady on Her Departure":

> Star of the North farewell - thy brilliant ray
> Shall happier skies illumine - O restore
> To us thy lustre, visit us once more
> Our life, our light, our day.

The two brothers also collaborated on a set of verses for Elizabeth, the engaging "A Perfectly New Chorus...".

———

After their marriages the relationship between the brothers remained cordial and trusting. Charles and Fanny moved to Caenby Hall, about thirty miles from his brother at Somersby, but within easy reach of his father at Tealby. George's letters to his brother are a touching mixture of family affairs (he and Eliza had eleven children and Charles and Fanny six) and intellectual and bibliographical discussion - Charles, too, was a great collector of books;[2] they display an (obviously shared) sense of humour, a boyish exuberance and a genuine concern, as in this example of December 1812:

> My dear Charles
> It much grieveth my inwards that I cannot be with you upon the first of January for two reasons
> 1st. That the first of January falls upon a Friday
> 2dly. That Eliza is not yet confined.
> These arguments are cogent and irrefragable. Not but that my bowels yearn much in brotherly love towards Caenby & more especially towards the Roma Antiqua & Moderna which you promised me when I came again, sed parcis submittendum or as Juvenal [sic] says Infandum regina jubes &c. You were a great black guard not to come to Somersby as you promised, the last time you

[1] T.R.C. N 15.
[2] See for example L.A.O. 2T.d'E. H78, Charles's library catalogue made in the late 1810s and early 1820s; only letters A and B are fully indexed.

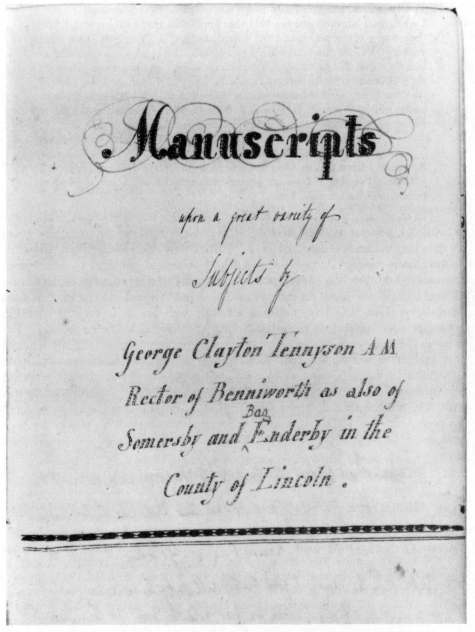

*Manuscripts*

*upon a great variety of*

*Subjects by*

*George Clayton Tennyson A M*

*Rector of Benniworth as also of*

*Bag*

*Somersby and Enderby in the*

*County of Lincoln.*

Figure 3: Title-page of George Clayton Tennyson's Commonplace Book (Tennyson Research Centre Collection).

were at Louth, but you fancy that I will submit to every outrage. I see in Lackington's last catalogue for 1811 that Lord Macartney's Embassy to China (large paper & the plates) sells for nearly nine pounds. You have fallen upon your legs. Jackson the bookseller, I find from Lackington's catalogue to be an infernal rogue, & I caution you by no means to buy anything more of him. In short all country booksellers are rascals. Babbington of Horncastle has charged me always one fourth more sometimes ½ more than Lackington sells the same editions for, I abjure all of them as a set of swindlers. Eliza's love & mine to Fanny, yourself & babs & believe me in haste (more paterno)

Your's very affectionately<br>G.C. Tennyson

P.S. When Eliza is confined I have no objection to spend a day or two with you but I should not like to leave her before the fortnight's end, & I should wish to be certain of your being at home.[1]

In these early years the two families spent much holiday time together at the increasingly popular (and populous) bathing stations on the Lincolnshire coast. Despite later coldness, Alfred and young Charles were as children particularly close to their eldest cousin, George Hildeyard, whose childhood coincided with the rise in fortunes of both brothers - before the later disparity in their material success drove George into defensiveness. As early as 1813 George Hildeyard showed the first signs of epilepsy: 'Our little boy continues tolerably well but he is very nervous and subject to constant periods of languor', Charles informed his father in May. 'The other day, Fanny was apprehensive, from an appearance which he suddenly assumed that another fit was coming on.'[2] Concern for his nephew's health was no doubt uppermost in George's mind when he wrote shortly afterwards about a proposed sea-bathing expedition, though he is also all too aware of the shortage of what he still calls, with student afflatus, 'spare rhino'. He is as always undisguisedly bitter about his profession's low social standing. Cleethorpes is now beyond his means as a poor parson:

I have consulted with Eliza respecting our journey to Clea, and [... thi]nks the water there will not be so salutary to George the [...] as that of the unadulterated sea. Another circumstance, and that which with me has great weight, is the insufferable expence of going there with a family, which will not

---

1  L.A.O. T.d'E. H66/24. George confuses Juvenal with Virgil (*Aeneid* II, line 3).
2  L.A.O. T.d'E. H71/54, 28 May 1813. There was much concern about George Hildeyard's health in this period, and he was frequently taken to bathe in the sea. In 1817, having left him with Fanny at Brighton, Charles wrote to his father; 'My thoughts run very much on this dear child, but my heart grieves while I endeavour to reconcile myself & poor Fanny to the idea of losing him. We must do our best for him and trust in God for the rest.... At any rate the thing is at some distance and I entertain much hope that by paying the utmost attention to him we may save him to be a blessing to us and an ornament to human nature' (L.A.O. T.d'E. H75/16, 5 June 1817). In 1819, he informed his father that Mr Cline, who had seen George Hildeyard 'during that frightful attack which he had in his head... thinks that with care & attention no mischief but perhaps much good will ensue from [sea bathing].... *All he ails is debility*, partly occasioned by rapid growth & partly consitutional' (L.A.O. T.d'E. H82/70, 21 August 1819).

at all accord with the ebb of my finances. These considerations have induced us to resume our original project of visiting Saltfleet, or perhaps Mablethorpe, which I understand is also a very oeconomical place. A poor parson with a house to build & furnish cannot be supposed to have any spare rhino to sport away in extravagant expeditions. I am sorry that squalid, blear eyed, ragamuffin goddess necessity should thus prevent us meeting you at Clea.[1]

Despite his sense of undeserved poverty, George's letters positively crackle with energy:

Mars, Bacchus, Apollo, Virorum being at present infaust, i.e. being in the 55th. Cusp of the ♈ house, absolutely impede our meeting at Clea. You will see I go up to Cambridge on the 21st. of this month... how then can I be at Clea on the 7th. & stay a week according to your modest proposal; forgetting as you do also the Pelion upon Ossa with which I am loaded. But howsoever, howbeit & nevertheless I expect you at Cambridge.... You see distinctly I cannot meet you at Clea, so don't be bumpseous....

I know Fanny will abuse me & say I don't wish to have her, but she is very much mistaken & if she will go I will send the carriage as far as Louth for her, where it can be met by your horses.[2]

Charles apparently changed his plans and agreed to come to Mablethorpe, for later in the summer George was busy with arrangements for a joint holiday. His letter to Charles gives a vivid and detailed picture of social conditions and expectations, and particularly of the gulf fixed between the gentry and their servants:

I received your first letter by Belwood & I immediately began to make a more diligent enquiry with respect to lodgings (for I had made enquiry before) but to no avail. Every potbellied grocer, & dirty linendraper bespeaks his lodgings from year to year & they are therefore preengaged throughout the season. At last I got the refusal of a very comfortable house near the sea, upon the departure of the lodgers, & I was going to write to you, when the man to whom the house belonged came & said that the Brackenburies who came to his house every year had written to him that they were coming & he could not disoblige them. This was very scurvy treatment & I think an action would lie against him; what think you & d——n the lousy race of Brackenburys thro' all its branches & from end to side.

There are no lodgings to be had at Sutton - every dirty cottage runs over. At Trusthorpe a small village near Mablethorpe, where I went yesterday, every miserable shed is occupied, by the aforesaid greasy & potbellied grocers & linendrapers. As for the inns you cannot be at all decently accommodated in them. They are stinking filthy places, not fit for a pig, & at Sutton a bed ridden person has existed in the kitchen amongst the cooking (a most cleanly circumstance) for the last twenty years. They are besides hyperextravagantly dear & according to my calculation, had we gone there, it would have cost us at the least £100 per Month. So far for the black side.

---

1    L.A.O. T.d'E. H163/70, n.d. [?late May/early June 1813].
2    L.A.O. T.d'E. H144/180, n.d. [?June 1813].

About a mile from the sea, at Mablethorpe there is a very nice cottage, with a very comfortable parlour, also a good bed room & good bed for yourselves with a fire place, Another good room with bed & fire place for a nursery. There is another small bed room in which the woman of the house & her servant sleeps; & therefore your man servant, if you come must have a bed made up for him in the kitchen which will be taken away in the day. This seems to me the best way of contriving & is the only plan I can devise. For I think you would not like the woman of the house & her servant to sleep in the room with little George, this warm weather.... Little George can bathe with our children & I have a covered cart on purpose to take them to the sea & for them to dress in.... Eliza unites me in best love to Fanny yourself & fry....

Mrs. Scamblesby has a very large long box into which she will put a bed in which little George may sleep very comfortably if you don't like him to sleep with the servant. The beds are all well aired.[1]

In 1813 George's life seemed, externally at least, to be rich and fulfilling. He became, in February 1813, no doubt through the influence of his father, chaplain to the High Sheriff, George Robert Heneage, and was expected to preach the Assize Sermon; he turned at once to Charles for help:

I was crushed all into a jelly when I found that the Assizes were appointed so early. I have not yet begun my sermon & am in a most horrible stew. I have ordered a silk gown & cassock in which I shall cut a most glorious appearance.

Following a lengthy outline of his sermon, he concludes:

I will leave a blank side. Write something for me & I will put it on the blank side. Especially do not forget a grand encomium upon law, which you are best qualified to write. I can myself write upon the day of Judgment. If you can rub administration so much the better. I think it might be done by referring to Sir Samuel Romilly's endeavours to amend the criminal law. This I will leave to you. Goodbye. Love to Fanny. Great hurry.

Your's luvingly
G.C. T————
I have not thought of a text, look over a bible[2]

George's letters to his father, in contrast to those he wrote to Charles, are almost exaggeratedly respectful, as in the account of the Assize Sermon he wrote a week after the letter to Charles:

I will not fail being at Hainton on Thursday next according to your wish, and I will endeavour to be at Tealby tomorrow by dinner, but I cannot promise, as the taylor at Horncastle who is making me a silk gown & cassock in which I may appear very smart & shining at the Assizes, will not perhaps be able to get it finished before tomorrow night. At any rate I will not fail being at Hainton on the day appointed.

If I cannot get over to Tealby tomorrow, perhaps Charles could accompany you to Hainton. He was to write me a good encomium upon law, for which I

1   L.A.O. T.d'E. H71/18, 19 August 1813.
2   L.A.O. T.d'E. H71/47, 23 February 1813.

thought he was best qualified, & I have left a gap in my sermon for its insertion. The subject upon which I have written is a little intricate, but certainly unhackneyed. I have great doubt of its pleasing all parties as my mother compliments me by supposing. My fear is least it should be misunderstood....[1]

Charles's wife Fanny described the Assizes and her brother-in-law's sermon in a letter to her mother:

I think I never was so starved as on the Assize Sunday at the Minster, tho' it was very full. I liked Mr. G.T.'s preaching very much - it was an excellent Sermon - tho' not admired by all at Lincoln....[2]

Old George's response to his son's public performance is not recorded.

George's reference to the 'Pelion upon Ossa with which I am loaded', in his letter cancelling the Cleethorpes jaunt, was to the LL.D. he was working on for Cambridge. A letter to Charles is full of these plans and activities:

I take the opportunity of your servant returning to Caenby to say that I shall go to Cambridge on the 21st. June, not being able to delay my journey there to a later period, as I keep my Act on the 2d. of July, & have a Concio ad Clerum to deliver in St. Mary's on the 24th. or 25th. of June. I find it requisite also for me to undergo the process of cramming with respect to the form at least of keeping in the schools, as old Jowett is very particular in this respect....

Concern about Charles's and George Hildeyard's health jostle for attention with academic matters:

I am very sorry to hear that little George has been so very unwell & that you have had partly a recurrence of your former complaint. Perhaps a little relaxation, if you can contrive it, would be of service to you.

I find your little Justiniva of infinite service: but the red letters hurt the eyes considerably.

At this stage in his career, George can rise above his difficulties with exuberant humour. Even the heavy demands of the LL.D. degree are a source of shared amusement:

A pretty kettle of fish! O Gemini! I think you pretty well understand the intricacy & obscurity of hereditates. I know however the 3 first books of Justinian off by heart: the 4th which respects criminal law I am utterly ignorant of, & shall not read: either for Dr. Jowett, or all the race of Doctors & Professors from Thoth, Hermagistus, Sanchoniathon, & Zoroaster to the worshippful Golgotha.[3]

The degree was successfully completed, George became 'Dr Tennyson' and the two brothers made a pact to visit their alma mater together once a year.[4] Two years later,

1    L.A.O. T.d'E. H144/100, 2 March 1813.
2    L.A.O. 4T.d'E. H6/28, 28 March 1813.
3    L.A.O. T.d'E. H71/25, n.d. [June 1813].
4    On 6 May 1819 George invited Charles to the Cambridge Commencement in July: 'We have a strong Lincolnshire party - Raunsley, Trollope, Walls &c &c. We shall have no want of society & it is a pleasant thing.... I have a claim upon you, as upon your

Old George obtained (once more through his influence with Heneage), the Great Grimsby living for his son. Measured by the unreformed conditions of the early nineteenth century when plurality of benefices and non-residence were the norm, George was doing well. Further confirmation of this (outwardly) successful ecclesiastical career came in October 1817, when George was invited to preach the sermon for the annual Horncastle Dispensary Meeting (Fig. 4).

———

All, however, was not well. His family's concern over George's health grew. His mother's letters of the time are, as always, full of a maternal solicitude which survived her son's quixotic behaviour and her own worsening health. In March 1816 she wrote to Charles:

> Poor George left us on Friday much better in his spirits and appetite - but his complaint which does not exactly put on the appearance yours did - still returns upon him about once a week. On Thursday evening he sat with his head on his hand as though he were musing - when his wife observed "he is not well" - we spoke - he did not answer - we repeated - he made no effort to speak and was insensible - when he open'd his eyes they roled without meaning and then he spoke incoherently for a minute - this wandering of the intellect is alarming. When I described this affection to Mr Barton he said he thought it indicated catalepsy rather than epilepsy be what it may he should be careful to erradicate the cause as soon as possible. He has employ'd a Dr Bousfield of Spilsby who was a pupil of Harrison's - but his pills he is careless about taking - for he knows not how he has been affected - or that anything has been the matter. We have desired that he with Eliza will come again soon - I wish Barton to see him and that no time may be lost - he has suffer'd in this way ever since Mr Boucherett's death and when you saw him here he had had one of these fits in the night at this place but said nothing about it & it seems the only one he ever remembers.

Mary Tennyson touches, with appropriate tact, on her doubts about the cause of the illness: 'whether to attribute it to bodily weakness or too acute a sensibility I know not' and reveals the conspiracy of silence which up till then had shrouded the disease: 'I have never before mentioned this to you, nor have I to Eliza but I think you should no longer be ignorant of what everyone seems to know - I was fearful in your anxiety about Fanny your nerves might not be equal to it and desired Mr. Barton to say little about it... but indeed it is now going on too long.'[1]

Gradually and sadly, the burden of an ever-increasing family and the sense perhaps of being outstripped by Charles (building a successful career in the law and entering parliament as M.P. for Grimsby in 1818) also began to tell on George's over-sensitive nature. At some stage, possibly in the middle to late 1810s, George returned to writing in his Commonplace Book, but these new verses are darker and more unsettled than those he composed in the relatively relaxed and happy

---

suggestion I acceded to your proposal of going to Cambridge every year.... I shall certainly (deo volente & not being in the shades) be at Cambridge.... There is fine musick fine sights & alma mater' (L.A.O. T.d'E. H84/20).

1   L.A.O. 4T.d'E. H11 (unnumbered bundle), 31 March [1816].

OCTOBER 24, 1817.

# HORNCASTLE DISPENSARY MEETING,

## FOR THE YEAR, 1817,

OF THE FAMILIES IN THAT NEIGHBOURHOOD WHO SUBSCRIBE TO THE CHARITY, AND THE
WELL-WISHERS TO IT WHERE-EVER THEY RESIDE.

---

### PATRONESS.

MRS. G. TURNOR.

### STEWARDS.

THE RIGHT HONORABLE SIR JOSEPH BANKS, BART. G. C. B. P. R. S. &c.
PRESIDENT OF THE CHARITY.

REV. H. B. PACEY, D. D. ⎫
REV. G. STREET.   ⎬ GOVERNORS.

EDWARD HARRISON, M. D. TREASURER.

AT ELEVEN in the Morning, the Governors will meet at the Bull Inn, to audit the accounts of this Charity.

At HALF PAST TWELVE the Governors will proceed to Church, where a Sermon will be preached for the Benefit of this Charity, by the Reverend GEORGE TENNYSON, L L. D.

At TWO o'CLOCK the three Stewards and the Treasurer, will wait upon the Lady Patroness, to take her Commands relative to the Management of the Ball and Supper, the Nomination of a Patroness and Stewards for the ensuing Year, and the amount of Contributions necessary to be levied on the Gentlemen who attend.

At THREE o'CLOCK there will be an Ordinary at the Bull Inn, for the Ladies and Gentlemen, each Gentleman to pay for the Ladies he introduces.

At SEVEN in the Evening will be a Ball, in the Ball Room at the Bull Inn; Tickets, Twelve Shillings each, to admit one Gentleman and two Ladies, or as many more Ladies as the Gentleman pleases to introduce, at Half-a-Crown each.

At ELEVEN at Night, or as near that Hour as the Convenience of the Dancers will admit of, a cold Supper will be provided for the Gentlemen and Ladies who attend the Ball: no Gentlemen but the Stewards are to sit down at the Supper Tables until all the Ladies present have been provided with Seats.

The Stewards will attend the Patroness from the Ball to the Supper Room, and seat themselves on each side of her, to receive and obey her Commands.

Gentlemen are requested to apply for their Ball Tickets to the Expeditor, Mr. Sexty, and to signify to him the Names of the Ladies they intend to introduce.

Gentlemen who attend the Ordinary are requested to give their Names, and those of the Ladies introduced by each of them to Mr. Sexty, either before or immediately after Dinner, in order to facilitate the Collection of the Reckoning.

The Meetings will be held in future on the Day of the Full Moon in October, or as near that Day as possible, and it will be advertised a Month at least before that time.

\*₊\* Presents of Game from Gentlemen who are good Shots, and those who appoint Game-keepers, will be very acceptable; and it is requested that one fourth of the Birds may be sent undressed for Dinner, and the Remainder prepared for Supper.

Weir and Son, Printers, Horncastle.

Figure 4: Horncastle Dispensary Meeting handbill, 1817
(Lincoln Central Library: U.P. 927)

17

atmosphere of his early married life. The feverish rewriting of stanzas - evident in their effect on the page - suggests a mind under stress. The same section of the manuscript book contains sketches and plans of the Rectory (Fig. 8), builders' estimates, and a detailed drawing of a (?garden) wall, all possibly preparatory to the work he carried out in the summer of 1815 and in 1819, when, with the help of his servant Horlins, George further extended the cramped Rectory by building a Gothic style dining-room.[1] The dates are perhaps not without significance. Charles and Fanny had left Caenby in 1815 and had established themselves in London (from 1819 their permanent address was Park Street, Westminster); George's more fortunate brother-in-law, Matthew Russell, was ostentatiously remodelling, also in the Gothic style, Brancepeth Castle which he inherited in 1817 - a project in which Charles was deeply involved.[2] George was morbidly aware of disparities between himself and his relations. He seems perpetually aggrieved by the behaviour of one or other member of his family - a tendency he shared with his father, but exacerbated in his own case by the fear of continued epileptic fits and a sense of his own powerlessness.

Charles's letters to his parents, as in this example of May 1816, now occasionally complain of neglect by his brother:

> On Tuesday last Harrison the painter called here to enquire whether my brother was here or where, as he (Geo.) had called on him the day before (Monday) when he was from home & left his name & a line saying he was only in town for a short period & would not therefore leave him his address or something to that purpose. We have heard nothing more of him. Can you or my dearest mother account to us in *any agreeable manner* for his not even calling on us? I must say I was & am much hurt & shall be very glad to be relieved from painful feeling by any account of the matter putting it on a footing distinct from consideration personal to myself.[3]

---

[1] On 1 August 1815 Dr Tennyson advised his father, 'I am so very busy with my hay & building that I could not conveniently ride over to see you' (L.A.O. T.d'E. H114/112). On 11 June 1815, he had paid Louth corporation £3 'for materials from the old Town Hall' (L.A.O. L.G.S. BIII/3). The (now demolished) dining-room, according to Sir Charles Tennyson's research, was built in 1819; Martin, p.16, suggests 1820.

[2] See for example Matthew Russell's numerous letters to Charles from 1818 to 1821 describing work at Brancepeth (L.A.O. T.d'E H78-81 & 108). Matthew had employed John Paterson of Edinburgh (d. 1832) as his architect (Colvin, pp. 623-24).

[3] L.A.O. T.d'E. H144/118, 30 May 1816. John Harrison (d.1834) was much favoured by the Tennysons. He exhibited portraits of Charles at the Royal Academy in 1811 (Fig. 2) and 1832; of Mrs Fanny Tennyson in 1813; and of Elizabeth Russell's son William in 1828 (Algernon Green, *The Royal Academy of Arts. A Complete Dictionary of Contributors... from... 1869 to 1904*, 8 vols (London, 1905-06), IV, p.7 - the last work is catalogued under James Harrison). In 1805, John's brother Henry (below, p. 42, n. 5), exhibited 'Willingham Hall, Lincolnshire' at the Academy (Green, p.6). Willingham, only a few miles from Tealby, was owned by the Tennysons' friends, the Boucheretts; the Tennysons' patronage of the Harrisons may have originated at this time. The portrait of George (Fig. 1) could well be by John Harrison.

For the most part though, the bond between them still held, helped probably by the teasing, combative and semi-flirtatious relationship of George and Fanny. George writes (September 1818) of a recent visit to town:

> Got home safely on Saturday night with all my books which I am devouring.
> Eliza's best love to Fanny & hopes to see her with you on the tenth October.
> We will quarrel & scratch till not a bit of either of us shall be left....[1]

Fanny thoroughly enjoyed the liveliness and spirit of George in his sociable moods; Charles, overwhelmed by work, must have seemed humourless by comparison.[2] Writing to her husband from London in October 1818, she sends, 'My love to your brother', adding, with evident relish of his recent visit, 'No more romps for me until I see him again.'[3]

The general trend, despite this, was downhill. There are references in George's letters to drink in which, as in Coleridge's references to opium, there seems a suspicious tendency on the part of the writer to 'protest too much'. He writes to his father in February 1819, for example, that, 'having gone thro' a course of calomel I am able to sleep without the assistance of spirits, of which I can assure my dear Mother & yourself that I have not taken a drop ever since I saw you, being well aware of their ultimate pernicious effects tho' they may afford a temporary relief'.[4]

George, despite his recurring bouts of envy, took a keen interest in Charles's developing political career, writing to him eagerly against the Bill for Catholic Emancipation which the more liberal Charles supported, and following his progress closely in the press:

> You have been dumb for some time in the house but I see you opened your mouth on Friday last & as I understand it from the Times intend to dilate it still wider on Monday on the Bankrupts Bill.[5]

His boyish enthusiasm occasionally resurfaced and when Charles retained his seat in 1819, following the settlement of an election petition, George's congratulatory letter began 'Hurra! Hurra! Hurra!' and continued, 'What a set of rogues, villains, scoundrells & ragamuffins must the fellows be who swore before the Grand Jury at Lincoln....'[6]

1  L.A.O. T.d'E. H144/128, 22 September 1818.
2  Their marriage was also showing signs of strain: they were to live apart for many years.
3  L.A.O. T.d'E. H144/130, 10 October 1818.
4  L.A.O. 4T.d'E. H19 (unnumbered bundle), 6 February 1819.
5  L.A.O. T.d'E. H144/136, 27 June 1819.
6  L.A.O. T.d'E. H83/84, 18 February 1819. In the aftermath of the Grimsby election, when he was very much preoccupied with allegations of bribery, Charles was taken ill. In a letter of 14 July, he informed his father, 'On Sunday morning last I was seized with a violent vomiting & could retain nothing in my stomach until about 10 or 11 at night. The disorder was I suppose an obstruction between the stomach and bowels - what I suffered was very great & the complaint at one time assumed so serious an aspect that within one hour I was blooded, blistered, clystered, & (attempted to be) purged beside the continued & violent vomiting.' Four days later he reassured Old George, 'I had no fit, except a mere fainting when I was bled....' (L.A.O. T.d'E. H79/20, 25; also H77/5,

At the start of the 1820s came an event which in retrospect can be seen as a turning point in the fortunes of both Alfred Tennyson and his father: at Christmas 1820 George removed young Alfred, and at the following Midsummer, Charles, from Louth School where they had been miserable and stifled for several years, and began to educate them at home, in preparation for Cambridge (Frederick had been removed from Louth to Eton in 1818).[1] It may well be that some of the additions to his library made at the sale of the contents of Langton Hall in June 1820[2] were in anticipation of his planned role as tutor. There is no doubt that he took his task seriously and devoted long hours to preparation; however it seems equally clear that the family used his over zealous commitment to his sons' education as a convenient explanation for the physical and mental decline which was evident in the following years. It was easier to accept this version of events than to see clearly a deeply unhappy and self-tormenting man who resorted to drink because he could not reconcile himself to his own life. A famous letter of August 1820 amply illustrates the morose and yet awkwardly vulnerable nature of this insecure son brought up by a ruthless and judgmental father. The evidence of the elder George's tactlessness does ring true and the energy and attack of both father and son contrast strongly with the more emollient nature of Charles:

> My dear Father
>
> I find, to my great disquietude, that you have thought proper to attribute to my suggestion or instigation certain expressions which may or may not have been used by Miss Fytche reflecting upon your conduct as a parent. I utterly disdain to exculpate myself from this charge. I did intend to have visited Tealby, but an accusation so unjust, so frequently reiterated and so totally unsubstantiated has so far oppress'd my spirits and irritated my feelings that it is impossible that I can do so with any pleasure. With the sentiments you yet entertain and have entertained for more than twenty years, I cannot wonder you told Mr. Bourne you had not a spark of affection for me. The rude and unprecedented manner in which you first address'd me at Hainton, after a long absence, on your return from York (I quote your own words "*Now you great awkward booby are you here*") holding me up to utter derision before Mr. Heneage, his sons & Sir Robert Ainslie, & your language & conduct in innumerable other instances, many of which have made a deep impression upon my mind, sufficiently prove the truth of your own assertion. You have long injured me by your suspicions. I cannot avoid them for the fault is not mine. God judge between you & me. You make and have always made a false estimate of me in every respect. You look and have always look'd upon me with a jaundic'd eye, & *deeply and experimentally* feeling this, I am sure that my visiting you would not contribute

---

1 George Tennyson to Charles, 16 July 1818).
  Frederick had entered the school in 1814, Charles at Christmas 1815 and Alfred at Christmas 1816 (L.A.O. L.G.S. C/I).
2 The sale of the contents of Langton hall, including 'The extensive and valuable Library, consisting of more than one thousand volumes of scarce and valuable authors, in various languages' took place on five days, commencing 6 June 1820 (*Lincoln, Rutland and Stamford Mercury*, 19 June 1820). This sale (of Bennet Langton's library) has erroneously been described as taking place in 1806: e.g. *Tennyson in Lincoln*, I, p.xv.

to your satisfaction and at the same time would materially injure my own health and comfort. Conscious also that I am thrown into a situation unworthy my abilities & unbecoming either your fortune or my just pretensions, & resisted in my every wish to promote my own interests or that of my family by removing to a more eligible situation, Unaccountably kept in the dark with respect to their future prospects, with broken health & spirits, I find myself little disposed to encounter those unprovoked and sarcastic remarks in which you are so apt to indulge yourself at my expence, remarks, which tho' they may be outwardly borne, are inwardly resented, and prey upon the mind - the injustice, the inhumanity & the impropriety of which every one can see but yourself, & which in your last visit were levelled against the father of a large family in the very presence of his children and that father between forty & fifty years of age. I should not have proceeded thus far had you not by your unjust aspersions set fire to the mass which was already disposed to ignite. You may forget or pass off as a jest what penetrates & rankles in my heart; you may break what is already bent, but there is a tribunal before which you and I may speedily appear, more speedily perhaps than either of us desire or expect - there it will be seen whether you through life have treated me with that consideration & kindness which a son has a right to expect from a father, and whether (as you have been accustomed to represent me to myself & others) I have been deficient in filial affection & obedience.

After this excoriation, he ends as always,

> I am, my dear Father
> Your affectionate son
> G.C. Tennyson[1]

———

Old George referred only once to this unforgettable letter, in a terse subscription to a letter written to his son six weeks later; however he did at the same time settle £20,000 on George's younger children, in equal shares.[2] In his life deeds must surely be taken to speak louder than words. Despite his critical and peppery comments, George Tennyson until his death supported the large number of people dependent upon him fully and unstintingly. (It is perhaps worth noting that none of the Tennyson brothers, with the exception of Alfred and Charles, ever supported themselves.)

By the spring of 1822 George's health had been so far threatened by drink that he removed to Cheltenham. He reported on his condition to his mother:

> I fear you have been some time expecting an answer to your last kind letter. The fact is I was so very unwell before I set off from home, that I thought it could answer no purpose to send you a more unfavorable account of myself than I had done before. Eliza & I are both here; she is by no means in a good state of health & I have consulted a physician with respect to each of our cases. He gives me great hopes that the waters will reestablish my health & says that a schirrus has not as yet formed upon my liver, but that he could not have answered for the consequences if I had not immediately come here. We are

1  L.A.O. T.d'E. H144/142, 14 August 1818.
2  L.A.O. T.d'E. H144/144, 1 October 1820.

21

advised to stay here a month or five weeks....[1]

His sister Elizabeth and sister-in-law Fanny were in Cheltenham with him when the terrible news reached them of the sudden illness in London, and then of the death (probably from thrombosis) on 8 May 1822, of Elizabeth's husband, Matthew Russell. George comforted his sister and supported her in her grief in a way which recalled their old fondness in the days when she was his only Muse. With his parents, he accompanied Elizabeth to Bognor. On his return to Somersby, he wrote to her, 'You have indeed never been absent from my thoughts - to think that you are suffering now as when I left you & to suppose that there is no intermission to your sorrows would hurt me more than I am able to express.' He continued darkly, 'I am sorry to say, with respect to myself, that I have not experienced any great advantage from the Cheltenham waters.'[2]

By the autumn anxiety about George's health had spread through the family. Fanny wrote to her husband from Cheltenham in November 1822,

> I am really very sorry to hear your brother is so unwell, and I fear in an alarming state. Any accommodation in my power, I should be most happy to offer him, but I fear a bed in this small house is impracticable.... I apprehend his lungs are affected, and consequently this mild air might be of service, otherwise he is not perhaps aware, that the water is considered very injurious to drink at this time - poor man, I am very anxious to hear of him.[3]

The general level of concern expressed in the family correspondence suggests that this may have been a serious breakdown. George's mother implored, 'O may it please the great dispenser of events to restore this dear afflicted child to his former strength & health - as well also to a calm and quiet mind';[4] his father was making plans to relieve him of his teaching responsibilities by arranging for the children's education at various Lincolnshire schools and Elizabeth Russell volunteered to help. George once more journeyed to Cheltenham - accompanied on this occasion by young Charles. There he met Fanny once again. With her, and freed from family responsibilities, he could reveal the lively, clumsily affectionate, coltish side of his nature. Fanny wrote to Charles on 16 December,

> We are all tolerably well here (your brother better every day...) .... Your brother is not like the same man, his spirits are very good, and we kick up such rows, that I expect Captain Matthews will turn us out of the house, for rioting....[5]

On 19 December, she informed Charles,

> Your brother improves every day, and talks of leaving us next week. Charles too is wonderfully better of his astma. Your brother flirts away with Miss Taylor, who dined here the other day, and fine romping we had I can assure you. He is rather dull for want of a male companion. Old Cunningham bores

1   L.A.O. T.d'E. H144/149, 15 April 1822.
2   Beinecke Library, Yale, 18 June 1822.
3   L.A.O. 4T.d'E. H24 (unnumbered bundle), 9 November 1822.
4   L.A.O. 4T.d'E. H24 (unnumbered bundle), 9 November 1822.
5   L.A.O. 4T.d'E. H28 (unnumbered bundle).

him, without being agreeable....[1]

After George's departure, she mourned his loss:

> You cannot think how much I miss your brother. I really think my spirits have dropped ever since; he was so drole, agreeable, kind and obliging. We used to take long walks together, in short he became at least quite a beau, but I had much difficulty in making him so. You will be surprised to hear, he had a new suit of cloaths, hat, and boots, which I vowed to buy him myself, rather than he should appear in his nasty old school-master's shoes. He promised to write when he got home, but I have not yet heard; I hope he keeps well.[2]

George's health once he was at home continued to decline. Deprived of 'Society', he became a prey once more to melancholy. His mother expressed her anxiety in a letter to Charles of 22 January 1823:

> [I]t is greatly to be fear'd that a convalescent state is far from him - for he is fearfully circumstanced his nerves and spirits so very weak, medical aid he will not hear of - should you write to him dont mention his low state of spirits - this is the term Eliza his wife gives it - & nervous to a high degree. We will if we can get him freed from the noise of his children....[3]

Fanny writing to Charles on 3 February 1823 reflected:

> I am truly sorry to hear so unfavorable an account of your brother, he feared a return of indisposition after he got to Somersby - indeed so many boys to teach is really too much, and with his weak nerves, and delicate health I fear it will upset him.[4]

A Hamlet-like inertia seems once more to have once more overtaken him. In a letter to Charles of 21 January 1824, George refers to having 'neither strength nor spirits to go from home' and continues,

> I don't know whether Fanny is in London but I feel very much ashamed in not having answered her kind letter to me & after such a lapse of time equally ashamed to answer it. If she is with you will you make a thousand apologies for me to her. The fact is my spirits are very bad & I never set myself about anything that I can possibly avoid, so that it is a default of temperament and not of inclination. However I threaten sending her a very *long long* epistle one day or other. I am sure I have reason to thank her for her kindness to me & every attention when at Cheltenham.

The letter continues with a remarkably bitter attack on his sister Elizabeth Russell. Sadly, after the events of the spring and summer of 1822, George's old sense of betrayal returned; cut off from her sorrow, he felt cut off from her love. Eighteen months later he is criticising her, very much in his father's manner, but accumulating around the specific grievance all the general insecurities of his life in that obsessive way of his which hints at underlying mental instability:

1   L.A.O. T.d'E. H144/158.
2   L.A.O. 4T.d'E. H31 (unnumbered bundle), 6 January 1823.
3   L.A.O. 4T.d'E. H27 (unnumbered bundle).
4   L.A.O. 4T.d'E. H31 (unnumbered bundle), 3 February 1823.

I hear that Mrs. Russell is very gay at Brighton; her gaiety is no business of mine. When I last saw her I requested she would write to me but I suppose she is so utterly absorbed by amusement and the things of this world and its pomps & vanities that she either does not care or does not deign to take any notice of my wish. I think it is not the way I ought to be treated. I, who gave up the *express purpose* for which I went to Cheltenham the recruiting of my health, to administer to her solace & support, might reasonably have a line from her when I requested it. I say that I devoted my health & time & money to her (the time that I was with her cost me £30 at Cheltenham) and she little recollects when in a bad state of health (as indeed I now am), how she trespassed upon that health by being almost the whole night in my room for a series of nights. This I vow to God in the most solemn manner I have never recovered, my wife knows it as well myself; I was getting well but the mistime & agitation rendered the subsequent waters of Cheltenham of no effect. I did not think that Mrs. Russell had been so ungrateful & so callous. What makes the matter worse I believe I had been very ill & she had seen me so when I requested her to write to me. I am hurt perhaps more than I ought by this her indifference. But money I am well persuaded disdains the feelings and I suppose Mrs. Russell is not so superior to the rest of mankind as not to feel their paralyzing influence. You would seriously believe that Mrs. Russell told me, a little before her husband died, that my family could live well & be educated genteelly for £800 a year!!! She would put out my children to school, when in *distress*! This of course I refused. There is no repromise. She need not make it for I *could* not accept it. But *she is very careful*. I estimate her as she deserves. I have no communication with her but I by no means wish you to conceal that I think she has acted ill. The money I have expended on her account I wish you not to mention for possibly she might make some *humiliating* offer of repayment. Her indifference & I must say *ingratitude* has nettled me to the quick.

The only reason which she can alledge for this conduct is that when lately she offered to come & see us we had not accommodation. This I suppose is to cancel all former benefits. We are three and twenty in family & sleep five or six in a room. Truly we have great accommodation for Mrs. Russell & her suite. We have not the house at Brighton nor the castle at Brancepeth. I have enlarged perhaps too much upon this. Whenever I am well enough to see you in London I will. Whatever Mrs. Russell may think I feel I shall always feel that she has not behaved as a sister and *obliged* sister ought to behave....

He added by way of a post-script, 'I should be ashamed to mention that Mrs. Russell is obliged to me, had not I seen her utter indifference & neglect.'[1]

A letter of 1 February 1824 deserves to be quoted in full as it sums up well the tensions in this unhappy man. Here are the self-pity and introspection, the (prophetic) insight into his sons' talents, the flashes of humour and generosity which still, outside his immediate family, won affection for him, but which were almost always now overcast by clouds of melancholy. An almost adolescent vulnerability is ineffectively hidden by heavy sarcasm:

[1]   L.A.O. T.d'E. H144/159.

My dear Charles

I am truly sorry to find from your letter that you are so unwell. Is the complaint upon your nerves or some disarrangement of the bodily organs? Perhaps (in case of the former) the exertions in parliament supposing that you *would exert* yourself would tend to dissipate it. I would not if I had *any health* (were I in your case) relinquish its duties. But I am speaking without chapter & verse & do not know how you are affected. You speak of going to Paris. How happy should I be could I accompany you there*. I think it would give me something like health of which I cannot boast at present. Less application & a change of climate & removal from the harassing business of instruction would perhaps restore me. But I feel my powers of mind sensibly declining, & the attacks to which I am subject must necessarily injure the intellect. I have had two in the last five days. I have however some satisfaction in thinking that my boys will turn out to be clever men. Phoenix like, I trust (tho I don't think myself a Phoenix) they will spring from my ashes in consequence of the exertions I have bestowed upon them. I feel that a breach between Mrs. Russell & myself can do no good. I should only be considered as exacting an attention to which I had no claim. She is so much engaged with the world that she has no time to think upon me. It is human nature & ought to be pardoned. *Especially* it is the nature of those who are affluent. A poor country parson to be thought worthy of attention!! Let my former letter to you be buried in oblivion. I was indeed descending from my own dignity to make any complaint of her. Let her own conscience testify whether she has acted a sisterly part. Let nothing then be mentioned. I have my own ideas upon her conduct but I feel it is a derogation to myself that they should be made known to her. Thank you for all your kindness to Frederick & believe with every good wish for you & yours not forgetting my love to my mesmate Fanny.

Yours most affectionately<br>G.C. Tennyson[1]

* I am so netted in by the instruction of my family that I cannot.

On 5 March, he again wrote to Charles about the proposed jaunt, and his perhaps over-hasty attack on his sister:

Many thanks for your kind letter & your invitation to accompany you to Paris. But indeed were I not restrained by my churches which I could not get served during my absence, I feel that I have neither health nor spirits to undertake such an expedition. I wish you all manner of amusement there & perhaps you will give me a line during your stay. Mrs. Russell wrote to me about a week ago and if you are sure that you never said a word to her upon the subject of my letter, perhaps I may have been a little too hasty with respect to her. Will you be so good as to forward the enclosed to her....[2]

To judge from a letter of 1825 he sent to Elizabeth Russell, relations were once again restored. He again was able to relax and write affectionately to his former Muse - though there is something of the rectory school-master in his observations:

1    L.A.O. T.d'E. H144/160, 1 February 1824.
2    L.A.O. T.d'E. H144/161.

You do wrong to confess you are long in making verses, for no one would conceive it from the peculiar ease of the metre. You are not however singular: Gray hammer'd at his verses with great difficulty, and yet they have immortalized his name. Æschylus, the great Greek tragedian, with great difficulty once composed three verses in three days; a poetaster once came to Æschylus, and boasted that he had composed three thousand in the same time. 'Your three thousand verses', said Æschylus, 'will last only for three days, whereas my three verses will last for ever.' Your soliloquy is very beautiful, and so beautiful that I have transcribed it amongst my choice selections.[1]

———

George's fits were increasing in number and severity. Mrs Tennyson wrote to Charles in March 1825:

> [Y]our father tells me he mention'd to you the other day - your brother being *ill* how *much*, or to *what extent* I know not, he has had a very bad attack - a fit as formerly, & which lasted almost an hour - his wife wrote me she was in such a situation she did not know what to do - as he would have no [med]ical advice - & yet thinks he has water in the chest, - & says he feels it roll about - unknown to him she wrote & your father wrote immediately to Dr. Bousfield, to attend him as a friend and physician - Dr. Bousfield has been (as by accident to George) - he says he found him in a very disordered state, but he would not open to him or consult him neither did Bousfield say under what circumstances he was there - but says, so long as he will continue to teach his children, so long he will be disordered & recommended Cheltenham as always being of service to him - adding if he will not submit to medical discipline &c &c &c - there will be every reason to apprehend a fatal attack. The night which follow'd the day of the fit, his wife watch'd him after he had got to bed - when in a short time he call'd out "I am dying" or going to him - his face was contracted and she thought he was expiring, she held up his head & he breathed with difficulty - he revived and said in the morning he had had a better night than usual. In my letter to Eliza (his wife) I said if his nerves could support the excitement without harm to him she might sound him & if she saw it would be agreable to him to see us, she would acquaint us. I have not yet heard from her....[2]

Charles soon wrote to his father:

> I return you Dr Bousfield's letter. It indeed presents an alarming account of my poor brother. I have little doubt however that a removal to Cheltenham or any other place where his mind could disengage itself of the harassing occupation to which he is daily devoting himself & get it into new channels of thought & his body into more active exercise, would be very beneficial to him. I shall continue very anxious on his account until I hear further.[3]

A few days later he wrote once more to his father, 'Thro' Sir W. Ingilby I hear a bad account of my poor brother. Rawnsley has written to him saying that the fit was epileptic & that it has left him very weak.' He added by way of a postscript, 'Perhaps

---

1    *Memoir*, I, p.11 [no date other than 1825 is given]. Alas, the album George refers to appears no longer to be extant.
2    L.A.O. 4T.d'E. H33 (unnumbered bundle), 5 March 1825.
3    L.A.O. T.d'E. H144/165, 9 March 1825.

Rawnsley may merely surmise that the fit was epileptic. In describing the matter he says that my brother *"has had an epileptic fit."*[1]

In July 1825 George succeeded in taking Charles and Alfred to Cambridge to enter Frederick for St John's, only to be struck down by illness on his return home. His father reported to Charles:

> I was sent for to Somersby yesterday morning at poor George's request. I went & took Mr Fytche with me from Louth. We found him just recovered from a fit weak & feeble he wish'd also to have seen your mother but she was too unwell to accompany me to such a scene tho' Mr Barton assures me that he has great hopes she is becoming more convalescent. George seem'd happy to see me, said he hoped every thing would be forgotten that had been disagreeable between us & hoped also that I would be a parent to his family - and my dear Charles I am sure you know me well enough to conceive what I would say on this subject. My life will not be long of course, but when I am gone I am sure you will supply my place with as much feeling & more ability should your brother die before me. He mentioned your mother with kindness & has frequently mentioned you with affection.[2]

Old George immediately wrote to Mr Burton, the patron of the livings, advising him that he had visited 'my poor suffering son, Dr. Tennyson' finding him 'in a very lamentable state'. He continued,

> I entertain very little hope of his recovery. I have to request the favor of you not to dispose of the livings he holds under your patronage, till I can have the pleasure of personal communication with you. I don't wish you to give me any promise that you will not do so, I only wish that nothing conclusive may be done, till you & I have consulted on the subject. I am sure the request I make will not be to the disadvantage of you & yours.[3]

Elizabeth Russell expressed her concern to Charles, 'I fear our poor dear brother is a pitiable sufferer; but I yet think & hope his sufferings not of a nature to destroy him so prematurely - it is painful indeed to take a view, either a home or perspective one, of all the branches, as well as the stems of our family....'[4] Despite alarm in the family, George survived; but his mother Mary, also dangerously ill, died shortly afterwards on 20 August 1825.

Old George survived the sad loss and continued to support his difficult and needy family, despite intense provocation. In January 1827, for example, his elder son, with the breath-taking insensitivity of paranoia, combined a request for the money promised to pay Frederick's Cambridge expenses, with a howl of complaint:

> I have to regret the reason of my not visiting you as I had intended with some part of my family. I have been credibly informed that you make it your business to speak in the most disrespectful terms of me to every one & to one person you represented me as "the greatest lyar that ever spoke", and this you had said immediately prior to writing me a very affectionate invitation. How

1   L.A.O. T.d'E. H144/167, 17 March 1825.
2   L.A.O. T.d'E. H144/170, 22 July 1825.
3   L.A.O. 2T.d'E. H13/1, 24 July 1825.
4   L.A.O. T.d'E. H144/182, 28 July 1825.

you can think so ill of me & yet write so kindly is more than I can comprehend. I regret exceedingly you should continue to speak of me in so injurious and unkind a manner, as it absolutely precludes me from visiting you, when I know you harbour so unjust & unfavourable an opinion of me, neither can it be pleasant for you to receive me, a person, according to your description, of so despicable a character.[1]

His father endorsed this 'extraordinary' letter with his draft replies. He agreed to increase George's allowance from £750 to £1000 on the assurance 'that you will pursue proper plans of education for your children & that I shall be precluded from further application'. He returned to his son's attack which 'forbids all comment, your experience & knowledge of me as a Father & a friend ought to have furnished a ready contradiction to him who could so slander me & in whom you appear too well inclined to confide'.

The Doctor was now consuming laudanum, calomel and alcohol in large quantities and everyone could see that here was 'a noble mind... o'erthrown'. In April 1827 Alfred and Charles had their *Poems by Two Brothers* printed in Louth. Perhaps it was the increasing threat from his talented and growing family, whom he was still tutoring at home, that fed George's sense of persecution. Late in 1827 his behaviour became violent. A family friend, the Revd William Chaplin of Thorpe Hall, Louth, wrote to Charles on 10 October:

My dear Sir,

I know not how to express my sorrow & to feel it my duty to call your attention to your afflicted brother. You must know that he has long been most singular in conduct, & I am sorry to add is now dangerously disposed to his wife & children; & I dread the fatal effects towards some of them, which would consign him to perpetual confinement for his life. A coroner's verdict would declare him under the influence of insanity, should such a horrid death be perpetrated by him. His excessive habit of drinking bring on such repeated fits, that he is as deranged as madness can be described. However dreadfull to meditate, the requisite means to curb these horrid paroxysms must arise with his own friends, & the sooner they place him out of reach of such bad effects to his wife & children - the better. The children are alarmed at him & the wife is in the greatest fright both in day & night, & I may in truth say in daily danger of her life. I think he might be reclaimed, & his health restored, if under the care of Dr Willis - but as long as he is under the uncontroled power of liquors, daily dangers await him & he may be consigned to imprisonment for murder under the influence of insanity. I think his physician Dr Bousefield of Horncastle (a clever man & late pupil to Dr Harrison) would have no difficulty in giving a certificate that he is in such a state, that he is not responsible for any act he may commit. The more I consider his dreadfull state the more I am alarmed for him & his family - he will not allow them to go to school, & he will not clothe them & what must be the end of all this for he cannot educate them himself. I am confident the greatest necessity now exists that his own friends must come forward, & stop so much evil & such impending dangers. It would be cruel to expect your father to undertake such measures, as are now

[1] L.A.O. T.d'E. H148/1a, 22 January 1827.

requisite, but I hope you can discover some friend able to take the arduous task, & let prompt steps become prevalent. His duty is sadly neglected, & his fits have come on in the church, so every one is afraid of him - & neglect the church.

The only person having influence with him, is a faithfull servant, a *coachman* - he can stop some violent paroxysms but that cannot last long - he will not pay any house bills, nor allow necessary food for his family. I am sorry poor Fytche by long bad health is unequal to such a scene, as that at Somersby - he has been at Harrowgate & Buxton & is worse for both. Nobody knows where George hoards up his money, he pays nobody. I shall be glad to hear that you devise some plan of safety to all, & believe me

Yours truly<br>William Chaplin

Old Mrs Fytche & her daughter have been to Somersby & are confident that some very early steps are requisite to prevent perpetual & evil consequences. Mrs Tennyson cannot get the children away, & will not leave them - she has spent a most dreadful life for some years. George's violence is well known in all the adjoining villages & his horrid language is heard wherever he goes. He has no judgement left or control over his tongue.[1]

Charles was alarmed but at this stage sanguine, '[T]he more I reflect on the subject the more hope I entertain that Mr. C.'s statement has no sufficient foundation altho' I am aware that at times my brother's indisposition presents painful appearances.'[2] He consulted Dr Bousfield, whose very different experience of George shows how well the Doctor could, again like Hamlet, counterfeit insanity - or perhaps in this case he is counterfeiting sanity?

In consequence of your letter received on Monday, I yesterday rode over to Somersby. A mutual friend of Dr. Tennyson and myself, from a distant part of the country, was engaged to dine with him, and I volunteered myself as his companion. I found Dr. Tennyson, except complaining more than the rest of the company of heat, as well as I have usually seen him of late, and in an argument which took place after dinner displaying the same acuteness of mind and playfulness of manner as when I first met with him more than thirteen years ago. A slight indisposition, however, of the eldest daughter, for which she wished to consult me, gave me an opportunity of seeing Mrs. Tennyson alone, and I found that she really does labour under the apprehensions at which your letter hinted, from the violent state of nervous irritation which breaks out occasionally in her husband. It is more however on her children's account than her own that her placid disposition appears so greatly unhinged. I do not make out that Dr. T's fits have of late been unusually frequent, or that excess in spirit drinking has been more than occasional. He habitually indulges too much in malt liquor, to which he has been gradually led by its soporific quality, having been always tormented by sleepless nights. Although in ignorance of what may be the result of this letter, I am sure I need not urge that the most gentle and

1   L.A.O. 4T.d'E. H39/15.
2   L.A.O. 4T.d'E. H39/2, 17 October 1827.

delicate means only could have any favorable effect on Dr. T's unfortunate malady. All reasoning would, I fear, be inefficient, and any personal restraint uncalled for and productive only of more painful consequences. A temporary removal from objects connected of late with so much distress and agitation would afford the fairest chance of recovery. A continental tour of a few months would, I confidently hope, return him to the bosom of his family restored in a great measure to both bodily and mental health, and capable of enjoying that happiness which a most promising and highly-gifted set of children should naturally produce.[1]

Charles had hoped that his father would not be informed of the situation at Somersby. However, Eliza's family, the Fytches, were concerned for her safety, and on 24 October Mrs Tennyson's sister, Mary Anne Fytche, sent a copy to Old George of the 'letter of remonstra[n]ce' she had sent to Dr Tennyson:

In consequence of the severe illness of my brother, & the infirmities of my mother, the painful task devolves upon me to remonstrate with you on the unparelled [sic] barbarity of your conduct to dear Eliza. Surely it was sufficient misery to be subject to the caprice of so dreadful a temper as yours for twenty two years without having her character vilified where she has no means of justifying herself. You have deprived her of all authority in the family, & encouraged the servants to insult her, she is not allowed to have any money, & if she asks for some for the necessary expences of the family, she is refused in such language as I should be ashamed to transcribe. These circumstances are so public that your poor children here are told of them every day by their schoolfellows; and we should consider our selves as accessories in your violence did we neglect any means in our power to deliver Eliza from such brutality. I once thought very highly of your disposition but the wilful continuances in one known Sin, has effaced every trace not only of noble feeling but of common humanity.[2]

On 30 October Eliza reported to Old George

I fear we cannot have the pleasure of visiting you at Tealby at the time you proposed as George will not allow any of the children to come with me nor will he let me have the carriage unless I promise to remain from home half a year a condition which of course I cannot comply with as I dare not leave the children with him. It was my intention to have accepted your kind invitation for a few days only as I cannot leave home for any length of time on account of poor George's violence which I fear increases. We had a terrible evening on Sunday. I wish very much to have some conversation with you & shall be happy to see you at Somersby as soon as is convenient to yourself. We can offer you a small aired bed & also my brother should you think proper to bring him with you. I will write to him on the subject to-day. Or (if you prefer it) I will meet you at my brother's on any day that you will please to appoint....[3]

[1] L.A.O. 4T.d'E. H39/1, 17 October 1827.
[2] L.A.O. 4T.d'E. H39/18. Arthur and Horatio Tennyson were then at Louth School (L.A.O. L.G.S. C/I) and lodged with their Aunt Mary Anne.
[3] L.A.O. T.d'E. H148/4.

Doctor Bousfield's recommendation of travel as a way of restoring the doctor's mental stability seemed to suggest the only solution. Charles therefore took his brother off to Paris for a few weeks. Elizabeth Russell had observed perspicaciously of the whole family that 'locomotion is the only thing I believe for spirits like ours when depressed & fixing exclusivel[y] upon one subject, I know this from [ex]perience'.[1] The subsequent improvement was short-lived. In March 1828 the Somersby cook accidentally set fire to her dress and died in a few days of burns. The Doctor was widely blamed for the tragedy. Tensions with Frederick, always the most aggressive of the boys, came to a climax when he was rusticated from Cambridge. In late February 1829 his father threatened him with a knife. Frederick escaped and planned to set off for London to read for the Bar. Eliza, who witnessed the events at the Rectory, expressed her feelings to Old George:

> You cannot but understand Sir that when I express my sentiments on this subject more strongly than I am accustomed to do, nothing but the urgency of the case could have induced me so to do, & that I should be the last person in the world to act as a principal in an affair of this kind had it been possible for us to accommodate our differences in any other manner. Having I think furnished a proof by submitting patiently to the life I have led for more than twenty years that matrimonial obligations were in my eyes of far greater importance than mere personal considerations. But when insult is aggravated by injury the burthen of such accumulated ills is grievous & insufferable. I shall take lodgings at Louth as soon as possible....[2]

Left alone in the rectory, George sank irretrievably into depression. On 12 March T. H. Rawnsley, rector of Halton Holegate, informed Charles:

> I think it prudent, to let you know that my old friend the Doctor is here, under the most deplorable state of mental depression and wretchedness. The scenes we once before lamented, & which I was in hopes would never more return, have been acted again, at Somersby, with the addition of a very unfeeling part, performed by the eldest son. The whole family quitted, and the Doctor was left alone & so ill, that his neighbour sent an express for me, fearing he would sink under his depression, and epileptic tendencies. When I arrived on Monday, I found your brother *feeding upon himself*, and most miserable....[3]

Rawnsley took him to his parsonage. After a few days George returned to Somersby and then travelled to Tealby. His father and brother, in desperation once more, arranged for him to return to Paris, this time alone. On 12 May he wrote to his father from London about his planned departure,

> I have made a codicil to my will in which all your suggestions have been attended to, & I have transmitted to you a power of attorney to enable yourself and my brother to act either jointly or separately during my absence. I will write to you when I arrive at Paris, but I cannot leave England without

1   L.A.O. T.d'E. H144/182, 28 July 1825. In a letter to Charles of 12 November 1844 she again advised 'Locomotion seems very favorable to some constitutions....' (L.A.O. 2T.d'E. H38/21).
2   L.A.O. 2T.d'E. H86/19, 27 February 1829 (*Letters A.T.*, I, pp.29-30).
3   L.A.O. 2T.d'E. H86/22 (*Letters A.T.*, I, pp.31-32).

expressing to you my most grateful acknowledgements for all the trouble I have given you & all the kindness you have shewn me, & my most fervent wishes that during my stay abroad you may enjoy uninterrupted happiness & health.[1]

The incident of the codicil (made that day) recalls earlier events when Old George 'disinherited' his eldest son: George altered a bequest to his eldest son, Frederick, in favour of his second son Charles (he also removed John Fytche of Louth as co-executor with Charles).[2] On 24 May, he again wrote to his father, announcing he had arrived in Paris 'on Tuesday evening last':

I have found in the Marlhions, our old friends here, every thing that is affectionate and attentive, & were I not harass'd by distressing feelings respecting my family I should feel much satisfaction & comfort in residing here some time as I have had no return of the spasms on my chest, and am in the midst of very cheerful society. But tho' I feel that I have been treated most indecently by them, I cannot but take the most lively interest in their welfare. Have you seen or heard of them lately? I feel most happy that you are so near them to admonish and direct them, and whatever you may determine to be proper for any part of them in regard to professions, &c &c will meet with my most hearty concurrence; & I trust you will not be opposed by them as I have been opposed. My wife wrote to me when I was in London but as she threw all the blame upon me and none upon herself, I have not thought proper to answer her letter. Mrs. Russell and the Hamiltons are here.... I shall take care to avoid them if possible....[3]

There was a suggestion that Charles might go to Boulogne to see his brother, but it is clear that by 6 July when George wrote to Charles, his sense of insecurity and of being unloved had once again returned:

I am setting off for Geneva today if I can find a coach. I have *positively waited for you three weeks in Paris*. You have never written to me mentioning when you were likely to arrive here & this has prevented me writing to you as I thought you might be here and so might not receive my letter. I have never seen the Hamiltons nor Mrs. Russell. I called last night at the Marlhions and Mrs. H———n was there when I retired without seeing her. I dare not trust myself in slanderous company. It annoys me much that you do not come here. I was cogitating that we might have made a little party to Geneva, stopt there about three weeks, seen the glaciers &c. Why you have not dropt me a line during your correspondence with Madame Marhlion [sic] I cannot conceive. Love to all chez vous. I will write to you either from Lyons or Geneva.[4]

On 31 July he wrote to Charles from Geneva, thinking it 'incumbent upon me to inform you of what I am doing & where I am':

I will not attempt to describe the beauty & sublimity of some of the scenery. It would beggar all description & neither painter nor poet could do a thousandth part of justice to it. You will I hope excuse me for not having written before. I

---

1   L.A.O. 2T.d'E. H86/39.
2   L.A.O. L.C.C. Wills 1831/228.
3   L.A.O. 2T.d'E. H86/43.
4   L.A.O. 2T.d'E. H86/61, 6 July 1829.

have been up occasionally four nights without intermission. Frequently two. When the body is very much fatigued the mind cannot act. But I have endeavoured to dissipate all mental feeling by violent exertion & the inspection of foreign manners & scenery. It will not do. I feel here as an isolated being, an outcast from England and my family. I frequently think of returning to England to have at least some familiar faces about me & to hear a little of my native tongue. At Berne where I was ill I felt the misery of not being able to make myself understood, for almost everybody talks German at Berne, & there was not even a French domestic in the hotel. I should wish very much to hear from England & of the health of you all & of my family.... I am very uncertain in my movements & a mind ill at ease is generally so....[1]

He added by way of a postscript:

I keep a journal & some of my observations on the manners & costume of the people where I have occasionally sojourned may perhaps amuse you on my return. I am very desirous of doing so, but it will be of no avail, as Mr Fytche & Mary Anne Fytche have encouraged my family to act in open rebellion against me & I suppose they still encourage the same feelings against me. Mr Fytche may perhaps have some time or other rebellious children himself & he will then be able justly to appreciate his own nefarious conduct towards me.

This last European journey, a sad, strange echo of the Russian adventure of 1801, turned into a mad flight by the Doctor from the darkness of his own soul and from Death. The hectic letters home are reminiscent of those of Yorick in *A Sentimental Journey*. (Sterne too was fleeing from Death.) Surreal outpourings, observations on Vesuvius, the Elysian Fields, the River Styx, seem poignantly to demand a sympathetic audience. In retrospect the letters seem the last flaring up of a brilliant mind before extinction, though they are intermingled with the familiar complaints of family neglect as well as of despair. Writing to his father and brother from Naples, where he sojourned for sixteen weeks, he observed,

No part of my family have written to me.... I wish [my dearest father] I were seated by your comfortable fireside, reading to you the paper in the evening, surrounded by faces familiar to me, enjoying a glass of your refreshing small beer, and seeing Sharpe help to prepare you for your morning's ride by buttoning your gaiters & yourself mounting your horse with alacrity to take your accustom'd excursions. Or with you my dearest Charles, your forehead furrow'd with East Retford case, enjoying Fanny's pleasant stories & harmless pleasantry, or romping with your daughter Julia....

Having thanked them both 'for the interest you take in my family' he made his adieu, adding, 'As for myself I feel that I have but little happiness to expect in this world & hope sheds but a very feeble ray.'[2]

The same sense of despair is evident in the letter to his old friend T. H. Rawnsley of 1 January 1830:

Would to God I was again in Lincolnshire. I envy your quiet & elegant retreat at Halton where you have the melody of birds to awaken you in the morning,

1     L.A.O. 2T.d'E. H86/71 (part printed *Letters A.T.*, I, p.42).
2     L.A.O. 2T.d'E. H86/80, 18 December 1829.

and not the perpetual screaming and dissonance which prevails in this city. You have your comforts and your friends around you & it refreshes the heart of man to look upon the face of an old friend. All about me here seems to be strange, & I feel a void in my heart, which no words can express....[1]

———

George returned to England in late June 1830.[2] His wife expressed her apprehensions to Charles, 'It appears to me there is but little hope of any permanent tranquillity. I cannot but confess I have the greatest dread of what may happen.... You know as well as myself that when under the influence of liquor, George is dreadfully violent.'[3] Restored safely to his family George seems to have spent the summer of 1830 drawing them again into his own fantasies. Young Charles ingenuously recounted to John Frere the tales of derring-do in which George once more attempted again to win his own approval and the admiration of those dear to him, to make himself the hero of his own life:

> My father has returned from his tour and I am much surprised to see him so well after the neck-break adventures he has encountered. On one occasion, proceeding along in a small carriage over the mountains, he was hurled down a precipice & stunned but saved himself from certain death by convulsively grasping a pine that grew out of a ledge: while the driver carriage & horse were dashed to atoms thousands of feet below him. Again, at the Carnival in Rome, a man was stilettoed in his arms, drawing, first, suspicion & then violence on his person: the excess of which he prevented by exclaiming that he was an English-man & had not done the deed. Again, he was suddenly seized with giddiness on the verge of a [pre]cipice & only preserved by the presence of mi[nd] of a person near him. At another [time], he was near being buried alive.[4]

Here is the eternal adolescent, the man who 'hath ever but slenderly known himself', to whom the role of wild adventurer was a desperate escape from the role he felt life had forced upon him, that of unloved, disowned outcast.

On 16 September he was sufficiently well to attend, with his wife, two daughters and young Charles, the Horncastle Dispensary Ball; a party from Somersby, including Dr Tennyson, was at the Stuff Ball held in Lincoln on 27 October.[5] The reprieve was not to be for long. On 28 December, George wrote to Charles congratulating him on his appointment as Clerk to the Ordnance:

[1]  L.A.O. 2T.d'E. H87/1.
[2]  Perhaps significantly when George returned to Charles's London home in late June, his brother, again, became unwell. On 17 July Charles wrote to his (ever anxious) father: 'This morning I have had a consultation between Mr. Gascoyne & Mr. Pennington a very eminent man who is said to have been very successful in all complaints connected with that which I have of late suffered from. As to the *Old Spasmodic Seizures* - no one knows any thing about that disorder - it is brought on by anything affecting the nerves - whether the cause be bodily or mental....' (L.A.O. 2T.d'E. H88/48).
[3]  L.A.O. 2T.d'E. H88/36, 5 July 1830 (*Letters A.T.*, I, p.45).
[4]  Beinecke Library, Yale, 27 July 1830.
[5]  *Lincoln, Rutland and Stamford Mercury*, 24 September & 29 October 1830.

I sincerely & heartily congratulate you on your accession to place & honor & emolument. I hope only that your health may not fall a sacrifice to the arduous duties of your office. I wish I might have seen you in your journey to Tealby. It was not much out of your road. As for myself I am ill & have been ill & the spasmodic astma has again attacked me. Under these circumstances, & in this cold weather, I am sorry I cannot meet you at Tealby....[1]

On 28 February 1831 Frederick wrote to his Uncle Charles:

My father has been seriously ill for some days & Dr Bousfield thinks him in great danger. He was attacked about ten days ago with a disorder of the stomach, which has been succeeded by a pressure on the brain & for the last two days he has been nearly in a state of insensibility. I fear this intelligence will be very distressing to you in itself, and particularly so , as you probably have at this time much business on your hands. But the crisis of his complaint seems to have arrived, & the next change is one of vital importance. We pray that it may, but we have little hope that it will *be for the better*.[2]

Dr Bousfield later (and tactfully?) diagnosed 'low typhus'; it was clear to all who saw him that the Doctor was dying.[3] On 15 March, Alfred wrote to his uncle:

All shadow of hope with respect to my poor father's ultimate recovery has vanished. Yesterday he lost the use of one side. It is evident that he cannot last many hours longer. It is a great consolation to us, however, that he is free from all suffering & perfectly mild & tranquil, seeming not to interest himself in anything that passes, which is the effect of pressure on the brain: the strength of his constitution has enabled him to resist his complaint a fortnight longer than his physician expected, during which period we have had many fluctuations of hope & fear: at one time we almost ventured to be confident that he would be restored to us: but that is all over now. We *must* lose him. May my end be as calm as his.[4]

On 16 March, unexpectedly peacefully, George died. Eliza, with typical warmth and good nature, forgave her husband everything, as her reply to her brother-in-law's letter of condolence indicates:

Your sympathizing letter was gratifying to my feelings. You do my dear departed husband justice in saying that he had an affectionate heart & amiable disposition & I hope that myself & family will endeavour to emulate his virtues. His errors were owing to the state of his nerves, which made him view every thing in a gloomy light & deprived him of almost every enjoyment of life. You might place on him the most sure dependence for he never betrayed his trust & had for you I believe the sincerest friendship to the last moment of his life. During the short intervals of recollection that were permitted him during his illness his mind appeared to be absorbed by the one thing needful & entreated us to pray for him. He mentioned your name Mrs. Russell's and Mrs. Bourne's a short time before he died but we could not make out what were his

1  L.A.O. 2T.d'E. H89/74.
2  L.A.O. 2T.d'E. H91/2 (*Letters A.T.*, I, pp.48-49).
3  There exists at T.R.C. a drawing by Arthur Tennyson (1814-1899) considered to be a portrait of Dr Tennyson in his final months (Fig. 5).
4  L.A.O. T.d'E. H147/3 (*Letters A.T.*, I, p.53).

wishes, as his recollection forsook him almost immediately. I trust through the merits of his Saviour his errors are pardoned & he is at peace for ever & ever & has found that rest for the weary & heavy laden which is never to be met with in this world....[1]

The Reverend Dr George Clayton Tennyson was buried in Somersby churchyard on 24 March 1831; T. H. Rawnsley officiated and six neighbouring clergymen acted as pall bearers. Of the Tealby family, only the Doctor's sister, the severe yet dutiful Mary Bourne, and his nephew, George Hildeyard Tennyson, were in attendance. His father, who had objected to an interment at Tealby, had gout and could not attend. His brother Charles was genuinely ill in London with sciatica and somehow had to be at the House of Commons on 22 March to support Lord John Russell's Second Reform Bill; his contribution, for the majority was only one, he informed his father, was crucial: 'If I had not gone - the Speaker's casting vote would have thrown out the Bill.'[2] His beloved sister Elizabeth Russell was in Hastings[3] and her daughter Emma would not even go into mourning.

To the Somersby Tennysons these were 'maimed rites' indeed. It was hot-tempered Frederick who memorably expressed in a letter to John Frere what all the sons, and particularly Alfred, the closest of all, must have felt:

[1]   L.A.O. 2T.d'E. H91/52, 28 March 1831. Charles's letter to Eliza is not extant. In a letter to his father of 18 March, Charles wrote of the 'afflicting news from Somersby': 'For many years past my poor brother has acted kindly to me. I think he considered me a friend - & I will do all in my power to justify that opinion by promoting the welfare of his family as far as I am able. He had a thousand kind & good qualities which would have contributed to his own happiness & that of others if he had not given way to failings arising out of a nervous temperament. I will not enlarge upon my own feelings - indeed it is difficult to describe them. I feel as a brother must - & I pray that a still severer trial may be long warded off from me....' (L.A.O. 2T.d'E. H91/34). See also Charles's letter to T. H. Rawnsley (*Memoir*, I, pp.73-74) for a similar expression of his feelings.

[2]   L.A.O. 2T.d'E. H91/49, 23 March 1831. This letter shows that Charles was deeply divided about whether to attend up to the last minute. His final, typically cautious, decision to remain in London was influenced by the state of his health and pressure of work in preparing the Ordnance Office estimates (L.A.O. 2T.d'E H 91/50, 24 March 1831), but must not be seen as a rejection of his brother. Old George had consistently advised him not to attend, only to relent when it was probably too late (L.A.O. 2T.d'E. H91/48, 22 March 1831; *Letters A.T.*, I, pp.55-56).

[3]   Elizabeth expressed her sentiments about the 'melancholy event' of her brother's death, though she admitted she had 'expected my poor brother's remains would be deposited by those of my beloved and lamented mother', in a letter to her father of 21 March: 'The shock upon my already feeble nerves, has been severe, though in a great measure prepared for it. I am however happy in the consciousness of never in the course of our existence, having said *one unkind word* to him or indulged *one unsisterly feeling*' (L.A.O. 2T.d'E. H91/42).

Figure 5: Pen and ink drawing by Arthur Tennyson, considered to be a
portrait of Dr Tennyson, possibly sketched in his final months
(Tennyson Research Centre Collection).

My poor father, all his life *a man of sorrow and acquainted with grief*, has come to that bourne from whence no traveller returns.... He suffered little, and after death, his countenance which was strikingly lofty and peaceful, I trust was an image of the condition of his soul, which on earth was daily wracked by bitter fancies and tossed about by strong troubles....[1]

On the night of the funeral it was Alfred who chose to sleep in his father's bed.[2] The gesture is an ambiguous one: perhaps designed to placate the poor ghost, it might also suggest a Hamlet-like shouldering of the burden of his father's unsettled wrongs, including a smouldering hatred for a wicked and usurping uncle. Certainly the shade of George Clayton Tennyson and the strange pattern of his emotions were to haunt his third son for years to come and to inspire some of his most powerful verse.

One final rite was probably enacted at Somersby in the months after Dr Tennyson's death. In the codicil to his will made in 1829 before his flight to Europe, George revoked the earlier bequest of his 'library of books' to his wife; he continued,

> I give to my said wife three hundred volumes of my printed books to be selected by her within three calendar months after my decease out of the whole library or books which shall belong to me at the time of my decease. And I direct my brother Charles Tennyson and the Reverend Thomas Hardwicke Rawnsley... to divide the residue of my said library, or the whole thereof if my said wife shall die in my life time or shall refuse neglect or decline to make the selection aforesaid, into three portions of parcels as nearly equal in value as may be. And I give one of such three portions or parcels to each of my three sons Frederic, Charles and Alfred. And I direct that my said three sons (beginning with the eldest) or some person on their respective behalves shall draw lots for the choice of the said parcels of books respectively....[3]

There is something wholly characteristic of George in this codicil - or coda - to his life. For him, the division of his library meant the division of his heart. This unworldly man of letters, forced by circumstances into the role of country parson and paterfamilias, turned back, before death, to his books, a ruling passion which in happier times might have made him a respected and successful scholar. It was surely no coincidence that George's Commonplace Book fell to the share of Alfred, the main inheritor and developer of his poetic talent.

---

[1]  *Letters A.T.*, I, p.56, 23 March 1831.
[2]  *Memoir*, I, pp.72-73.
[3]  L.A.O. L.C.C. Wills 1831/228.

# TENNYSON D'EYNCOURT

Whilst Charles agonised over whether he should come to the funeral of his brother, his son, George Hildeyard, reassured him, 'My grandfather desires me also to add that your future conduct to the Somersby family will convince the world of the substantial goodness of your heart, & will far more than compensate for deficiency in a matter of form.'[1] It was however not until the middle of May 1831 that Charles was able to visit Somersby to discuss arrangements for his brother's children. Charles, like any aspiring member of the Establishment, worried about the effect of his unconventional relatives on his own reputation. Earlier, in 1828, he had warned George Hildeyard, newly arrived at Trinity College, Cambridge, against the society of the three Somersby brothers.[2] Understandably, Charles considered ordination as a possible profession for Alfred. He wrote to his anxious father at Tealby:

> Alfred is at home - but wishes to return to Cambridge to take a degree. I told him it was a useless expense unless he meant to go into the Church. He said he would. I did not think he seemed much to like it. I then suggested physic or some other profession. He seemed to think the Church the best & has I think finally made up his mind to it. The Tealby living was mentioned & understood to be intended for him....

Within a few days Charles seems to have realised the true nature of his nephew's ambition:

> Alfred seems quite ready to go into the Church altho' I think his mind is fixed on the idea of deriving his great distinction & greatest means from the exercise of his poetic talents.[3]

In the years that followed, relations between the two branches of the family became strained. Following the searing reviews of Alfred's 1832/3 volume Charles wrote to George Hildeyard (who for much of the 1830s worked for the Colonial service in the Ionian islands):

> As to Alfred's Poems - some of them were good & some rubbish but I had not patience to read scarcely any of them. I do not & never did like his affected and lame style. It is perhaps want of taste - but I felt that the Quarterly Review was scarcely too severe.[4]

The same letter contains a possible clue to the severity of his attack on Alfred. He referred to the recent suspension of his son Eustace from Sandhurst following an

---

1    L.A.O. 2T.d'E H90/8, 22 March 1831.
2    'Your cousins are I doubt not very respectable young men & very clever - but *their habits* may be confined & their society limited. It is not that I am fearful of any improper conduct on their parts but do not, I repeat, suffer yourself blindly to be drawn into *confined muddling* habits.... Your cousins are very well informed on many literary matters & may be of use to you. Avoid all conversation (without seeming to do so) on family matters - otherwise, *it will & must* end ill, particularly with Frederick' (L.A.O. 2T.d'E. H23/31, 5 October 1828).
3    L.A.O. 2T.d'E H91/63, 18 May 1831 (*Letters A.T.*, I, pp.60-62).
4    L.A.O. T.d'E H116/62, 28 November 1833.

affray at Bagshot:[1] 'He is a nice excellent hearted high spirited fellow... I have no doubt he will do well if we can get him thro' his present difficulty, which has made a deep impression on him.' Charles, faced with the disgrace of one of his own children, could not tolerate the success of one of his brother's. This was to be the first of many problems Charles had with his family - he was often unwilling to accept his children could ever be in the wrong.[2]

———

Charles, however was frequently in London, and it was Old George and his grandchildren, who were directly involved with (and had the harshest words for) the Somersby family. He wrote to Charles in July 1832, 'I am inconvenienced & troubled more & more about my poor lost George's family' - adding that young Charles, who had just been appointed curate at Tealby, had discharged his first duty 'in the hubble bubble way of that family'.[3] Shortly before his brother's arrival, Frederick visited Bayons, and according to his grandfather (writing to his son),

> treated and left me in the most brutal manner. He is a savage. Sir William [Ingilby] and [Col.] Cracroft observed his conduct but did not see his brutality towards me. Mrs. Vane and Miss Gray did and they don't think I am safe near him. On his leaving me I said he would kill me by his conduct. His answer was, you will live *long enough*. I have been at Rasen to day and given instructions for an alteration in my will. He governs the whole Somersby family & said when you were there you acted so improperly *he* would take care you should not be admitted again. It is high time that house should be shut up. I only let Charles have one low and one bed room at Grove House so that he cannot entertain this brute.[4]

This was the second time Old George had 'disinherited' an eldest son. He continued to be inconvenienced and troubled by his Somersby dependants for some time: debts had to be settled;[5] Edward was placed in a private mental asylum in York at the end of 1832;[6] in 1833 Old George negotiated in an uncompromising manner with Mr Hallam about Arthur's marriage to Emily. The Somersby family showed little appreciation for his shouldering of their responsibilities. Alfred wrote to his Aunt Russell in March 1833, 'Of my grandfather I have seen little for the last three years, he has so rooted an antipathy to me from some cause or other that it is not pleasant to visit him without a special invitation.'[7]

1      For the affray at Bagshot see L.A.O. 2T.d'E. H28/13 & H29/4-33.
2      For an account of Charles's family see J. Murray, 'The Tennyson d'Eyncourt nicknames', *Lincolnshire History and Archaeology*, 27 (1992), pp.34-39.
3      L.A.O. T.d'E H111/62, 14 July 1832.
4      L.A.O. T.d'E H111/63, 27 July 1832.
5      Old George estimated the debts to be £1600, L.A.O. T.d'E H111/69, George Tennyson to Charles Tennyson, 13 August 1832.
6      *Letters A.T.*, I, pp.81, 83-84. Christopher Daniell, 'Edward Tennyson in York: 1832-1833', *Notes and Queries*, N.S. 34, 1 (1987), pp.32-35, and 'Edward Tennyson in York 1833-1890', *ibid.*, N.S. 35, 3 (1988), pp.315-17.
7      *Letters A.T.*, I, p.89, 10 March 1833.

Frederick eventually made peace with his grandfather. Young Charles, however, continued to be a thorn in Old George's flesh, arguing frequently about arrangements at Grove House. There was also great concern from c.1834 over his increasing dependence on laudanum - Clara wrote to George in April, 'I pity poor Charles who is almost killing himself with laudanum & suffering so much from lowness of spirits.'[1] Charles's great uncle Sam Turner (the non-resident incumbent of Tealby) died in March 1835. Charles declined the offer of the Tealby living, becoming vicar of Grasby, and moved to Caistor. Eustace expressed the relief felt, no doubt, by all the Tealby family: 'There is one good thing arising from poor Charles going to live at Caistor, for you will not then have the swarms of Goths and Vandals down upon you every week.'[2] As his uncle was to do in the same year, young Charles changed his name; under the conditions of Sam Turner's will he became for the rest of his life Charles Turner (and as a cleric became also the first member of the Somersby Tennysons to earn his own living).

———

By the early 1830s, Charles's graph of political success had reached its peak.[3] He had challenged successfully the Cecil family interest at Stamford in the election of May 1831 (in the aftermath of which he had fought a duel with Lord Thomas Cecil on 18 June at Wormwood Scrubs);[4] he was in the van of parliamentary reform. However, pressure of his parliamentary duties began to take their toll on Charles's health. Early in February 1832, he resigned his post at the Ordnance Office and was appointed to the Privy Council (in recognition of his efforts for reform).[5] Clara wrote to her father,

> I think I never saw any one more delighted than poor Grand Papa, the tears ran down his face & for once in his life declared that £1200 was a good loss & that it would prove a gain to you in the end....[6]

Julia expressed her relief,

> I am delighted that you have given up the Clerkship, & are no more a tired automaton, in the shape of a quill-driver, with a conscience, valued at £1200 a year but a fine Right Honourable Privy Councillor (how nice it sounds) with a tongue of your own to speak with, & a tooth of your own, (not a false one) to

1     L.A.O. T.d'E 116/22, 27 April 1834.
2     L.A.O. T.d'E H117/64, 29 March 1835.
3     For a summary of Charles's political career, see Joseph O. Baylen and Norbert J. Gossman (eds.), *Biographical Dictionary of Modern British Radicals. Volume I: 1770-1830* (Hassocks, 1979), pp.120-24.
4     For the duel see L.A.O. T.d'E H32 & 2T.d'E. H26.
5     But compare Thomas Creevy's comment (30 January 1832): 'Durham told me Tennyson is moving heaven and earth to get the name of his office changed from "clerk" to that of "secretary" or anything else, alleging gravely as a reason that a very advantageous marriage for his eldest daughter had gone off, solely from the lover not being able to stand the lady's father being a *clerk*!' (Sir Herbert Maxwell (ed.), *The Creevy Papers...*, 2 vols (London, 1903), II, p.241).
6     L.A.O. T.d'E H20/9, n.d. [?4 February 1832].

bite with, & when you have been taken into bait here, for a short time, I trust you will have two legs of your own, to stand upon....

[Grand Papa] has been making us search all the Red Books, & Calendars, & Almanacs & Peerages to see the precedence you take and to find a list of Privy Councillors.... I am so glad you were not made a peer, so many fools are made peers.[1]

Despite Julia's brave words, the lack of a peerage was certainly the greatest blow to Charles's political career; the Privy Councillorship was but poor consolation. The Somersby Tennysons, with pardonable relish, in later years delighted in referring to their uncle as 'The Right Dishonourable'.

Charles's health did not recover fully. On 17 February he informed his father that his previous letter had been 'written very late after a day of *worry anxiety* & *agitation* & when I was suffering from the ailment in my chest & every nervous feeling... I am not well - I have been overdone by an anxious mind'.[2] The same day he consulted Dr Farre:

He says that I must take care of myself - that I have done quite right in quitting office - that I have tried my mind & strength too much - that he believes at present there is no fixed mischief about the heart - & that if I act up to my purpose of sparing myself from anxiety & turmoil I shall gradually get right - but if not, (altho' he sees no present cause of alarm) it might become serious....[3]

Plans were made immediately to enlarge Bayons so that Charles could spend more time there (they would also ensure a house befitting the residence of a Privy Councillor!). Old George wrote to his son on 22 February enclosing 'the ground plan and elevation of the intended room. The elevation is bad. I think it should be of the Gothic or Abbey style, if the former Mr Willson would give a good design, but both as to the plan and elevation consult who you please and give me your opinion & taste.' Also enclosed in the letter was a plan drawn by Julia (but of Old George's ideas); she commented, 'I do not think it is what you will like - I should think projecting gable ends were more what you intend.'[4] Charles commissioned plans and elevations from Anthony Salvin (who had worked at Brancepeth in the 1820s) and Harrison, sending them to his father on 28 March.[5] Julia's letter to her father of 30 March made it clear that the scheme would come to nothing:

1   L.A.O. T.d'E. H20/10, 4 February 1832.
2   L.A.O. T.d'E. H111/7.
3   L.A.O. T.d'E. H111/9, 18 February 1832.
4   L.A.O. T.d'E. H20/6. For E. J. Willson (1787-1854), architect and antiquary, see Colvin, pp.898-99.
5   L.A.O. T.d'E. H111/17 & 18. For Salvin (1799-1881) see Jill Allibone, *Anthony Salvin: Pioneer of Gothic Revival Architecture* (Cambridge, 1988). Harrison was almost certainly Henry Harrison (c.1785-c.1865), who from 1828 to 1839 lived at 21 Park Street (Charles's London address), Colvin, pp.292-94. He was the brother of John Harrison, Tennyson's favoured portrait painter: on 3 July 1834 H[enry] Harrison wrote from Park Street advising Charles of his brother John's death (L.A.O. T.d'E. H1/25). In 1823 Henry worked for Charles at Park Street and visited Brancepeth (L.A.O. T.d'E. H89/63).

Grand Papa received the plans last night. He desires me to say that he has considered them, but that he would wait till he sees you at Easter to agree upon any. As to Mr Salvin's coming here, he would rather see his Black-Majesty himself, & says that if he consulted any architect here it would be Wilson of Lincoln - but that he is himself a better architect than all three put together. I think Mr. Salvin's elevation with Mr. Harrison's roof very pretty. *Any* addition to this gim crack house, must alter its character of a cottage & the height above the present roof will be like the Devil looking over Lincoln. I was thinking that perhaps the floor of the library might be sunk two or 3 feet below the surface of the ground but this would not do well inside. Grand Papa groaned & exclaimed lamentably last night but I have been for the last hour & a half explaining away some of his grumbulations. He said last night that all the plans were whimsicalities & Brancepeth Castle visions. He cannot see the use of a private writing closet, when there is *so much* room in the house. As to the *passage wall* downstairs, it is not required he repeats & it will only serve the purpose of darkening the book room, & this is one of his most *insurmountable* objections to this writing closet. When I recapitulated the advantages of the bay window, he *drummed* on about the window taxes & the extra expence, in short he cannot see that any improvements are wanted to his own plan in any way. But he is gradually coming round to allowing himself to like Mr. Salvin's elevation of the *west* side of the house - and much further I could not get him this morning but I have hopes of him. These are only private hints - Grand Papa only desired me to say that he would leave all till he sees you & that he did not wish for Mr. Salvin's company.[1]

Set against Julia's wit and charm (so reminiscent of her Aunt Russell) it is easy to condemn the cantankerous and dyspeptic nature of Old George; one must however give him credit for a level-headedness absent in the younger members of his family, all now caught up in the Bayons vision.

Old George continued to press his son to spend more time at Tealby away from the pressures of London. On 15 March he was assured by Charles:

As to my withdrawing in a degree from public life I am doing so by quitting office & by *taking my parliamentary duties easily* - & hereafter, at no great distance of time, viz. at the next dissolution of parliament, I am *quite ready seriously* to consider the expediency to withdrawing from parliament and public life altogether. This will depend on health & other circumstances - at the time, - & in the interval I am fully resolved to spare myself to the utmost.[2]

Old George became anxious about Charles's decision to accept an offer to stand after the passing of the Reform Bill for the new metropolitan borough of Lambeth:

I read your two letters as to Lambeth with fear and trembling, and I fear and tremble for the result let be it what it may as to success, for I am sure it will be an arduous undertaking and oppress and injure your health which above all things ought to be avoided... [T]he distant & harrying life you are likely to lead deprive[s] me of all hopes of your becoming a country, Lincolnshire, gentleman

1  L.A.O. T.d'E. H111/20.
2  L.A.O. T.d'E. H111/14.

during my life....[1]

Charles was elected member for Lambeth in December 1832.

Perhaps spurred on by the possibility of the Speakership (and consequent peerage), Charles began to consider reviving the old family name of d'Eyncourt. In January 1833 he wrote to his father,

> You will recollect all the abuse against our family. You expressed a wish that I would look into your claim to the title of D'Eincourt. I turned to my pedigrees & consulted my friend Sir William Woods of the Heralds college. He finds that we have a much finer pedigree than I expected... [W]e inherit the blood of the old Barons D'eincourt which title was however forfeited in the Reign of Henry 7th so that no one *can claim* the title or name (which is also extinct) owing to the attainder. This blood however you inherit through Jane Pitt & by a most illustrious descent from the ancient Barons d'Eincourt. But in addition to this you happen, by a most extraordinary coincidence to be coheir at law (through Christopher Hildyard the husband of Jane Pitt) to the *last Lord Deincourt* Earl of Scarsdale who died in 1736, & it is by reason of this descent that you quarter the arms of the Earl of Scarsdale....

He advised his father that Woods was assisting him to prepare a petition to the King (on Old George's behalf), 'to assume the name of D'Eincourt having already the arms of the last Barony of that name'. He urged his father to support him, adding, 'I really think it is a hit to make which should not be lost. It would be the most *compendious answer* to those who have been running us down & considering us as rubbish. The ancient D'Eincourts had their lands chiefly in Lincolnshire & were in fact a Lincolnshire family....'[2] Old George's first reaction was understandable:

> It would hurt my feelings to lay aside the name of Tennyson for this Frenshyfied name & should not I and we be laught at and held in derision for so doing? Besides I consider that our ancestors in the Tennyson line have been by profession and otherwise gentlemen, that the females in that family have done nothing discreditable, that the family have always paid their debts & none died insolvent. In regard to hanging a peerage upon the name of Deanycourt [sic], even suppose, it was granted on the retirement of a Speaker with a retiring pension of £4000 a year yet even this addition to the fortune *you* would have would not support the dignity. You say the expense of taking the name would not be much. What do you call much? You know we are circumstanced in money concerns and a little may be much to us. I suppose if the patent was granted to me and my issue - you and your family could take the name, am I right?

In conclusion he conceded, 'Now after all as it has ever been my wish so it ever will be to comply with your wishes so it is now & you may act in this matter as you think wisest & best for yourself and family....'[3] The petition was rejected by the

---

1   L.A.O. T.d'E. H111/45, 1 July 1832.
2   L.A.O. T.d'E. H114/1, 30 January 1833. See John Bernard Burke, *Genealogical History of the Family of Tennyson d'Eyncourt...* (London, 1846) included in his *Memorials of Bayons Manor...* (London, 1852).
3   L.A.O. T.d'E. H113/5, 1 February 1833.

Home Secretary, Lord Melbourne, in March; an appeal to Melbourne by Charles's nephew William Russell in April was to no avail.[1] Charles, however, persuaded his father to change his will once more: Charles's inheriting the manor of Usselby was to be contingent on his assuming the name d'Eyncourt.

In March 1833 Old George once again reminded his son, 'I fear you are now so immersed in politics, as never to think of the arrangement we consulted upon as to your residence here.'[2] Charles and Fanny agreed to the move in the summer (in compliance with Old George altering his will?), but it was some time before plans were finalised. Julia wote to her father on 30 July:

> It is totally impossible to bring Grand Papa to any steady consideration or sort of conclusion as to any arrangements with respect to our living here & I merely send you what I am able to gather from signs & appearances. He declares that he will not live either with or near Mama, & seems therefore quite averse to your having the house below, but seems to prefer the idea of *his* going either to Ussleby [sic] or Grimsby & your having this house.[3]

Only at the end of the year did he move,[4] with Julia as his companion, to Usselby. During February 1834 he was visited by Frederick who found him

> gone to live on a sandy moor. I should have supposed that such a thing would alone have been sufficient to shake the last sands out of his glass. My uncle's family are already installed in the squiredom, but such things do not make him like Lear to double his fist at heaven, or think the wintry winds nothing to it.[5]

Old George died on 4 July 1835. Fanny wrote to her son George Hildeyard, 'Poor man he had a hard struggle towards the last, but was very patient and resigned - it was very agonizing to your father. A short time previous to his dissolution he called to him and said "Charles I am dying, help me" and immediately seized your father's hand, which he grasped convulsively and died in that position.'[6] His funeral at Tealby was attended by some two thousand mourners, but not by the Somersby family. Perhaps the memory of Dr Tennyson's funeral was still too painful for them: whatever the facts, their feelings were still coloured by bitterness towards 'The Old Man of the Wolds'.

On 31 July, a Royal Licence was issued to change the family name to Tennyson d'Eyncourt. On 1 August, Edwin wrote to his brother George Hildeyard:

> I am very glad we have changed our name, as it gives us a good position, and if we had not my father would always have been Mr. Charles Tennyson. Besides which it will keep us in a great measure clear of the Somersby family who really are quite hogs. Not one of them came to the funeral.[7]

1   L.A.O. T.d'E. H3/3-9.
2   L.A.O. T.d'E. H113/11, 4 March 1833.
3   L.A.O. T.d'E. H113/30.
4   Edwin wrote to George on 28 October 1833, 'My father is at present not very well. My G. Father bothers his life out. He G.T. has settled and I really think will go to Usselby in about 3 weeks, then my mother will come here' (L.A.O. T.d.'E. H113/50).
5   *Letters A.T.*, I, p.108, 14 February 1834.
6   L.A.O. T.d'E. H116a/30, 30 July [1835].

Old George's will made appropriate provision for the Somersby family,[2] but relations between the two branches of the family declined further. Fanny wrote to George Hildeyard in August,

> I hear the family at Somersby are one and all, much disappointed at their *handsome* increase of property - but they expected more, and the girls very handsome fortunes besides - some people are never satisfied!! They also say, that *Frederick* ought to have taken the name of d'Eyncourt, as being the eldest of the eldest son![3]

Some mysterious, unspecified actions attributed to Alfred caused Edwin once more to express his feelings in September: 'Your letter to my Aunt [Russell]... has convinced me what a hog that Alfred is and what can you expect from a pig but a grunt... As to his not seeing me, I can assure him that I feel excessively grateful for his decision on that point, because I would rather be excused meeting a bloated ploughman.'[4]

Fanny returned to her attack on Frederick (who had been staying with George Hildeyard in Corfu when their grandfather died) later in the month: 'I congratulate you exceedingly, at your riddance of so great a plague in the shape of a relation, who has already arrived at home, and report says, is determined to take the name of Clayton forthwith.'[5] On 17 May 1836 (a week before his brother Charles's wedding) Frederick complicated family tensions further by declaring the love he had held 'since I was a boy' for Julia.[6] In her draft reply she wrote, 'I feel so thoroughly unworthy of the affection you offer me, that my heart bleeds at the idea of my hand being chosen to inflict a wound on one who deserves a better return than it is in my power to bestow. Forgive me, my dear Frederick but we must remain as we were & I hope the friendship which has ever existed between us will also remain unaltered....'[7] Nothing is known of Frederick's response, although, given the circumstances, he could not have been unduly surprised or hurt by this rejection. His subsequent departure for Italy removed one source of tension between the families of the Two Brothers.

———

Ensured of Old George's fortune, within a few months of his father's death Charles revived the project of remodelling Bayons abandoned in 1832. In August 1835, Louis wrote to George Hildeyard:

> As soon as my father comes down we shall be very busy with building a hall on the south side of the house. It is to be built of the brown stone of the country...

1     L.A.O. T.d'E. H116a/31 (*Letters A.T.*, I, p.135).
2     L.A.O. L.C.C. Wills 1835/326. See especially the discussion in Sir Francis Hill, 'The disinheritance tradition reconsidered', T.R.B., 3, 2 (1978), pp.41-54.
3     L.A.O. T.d'E. H116a/33, 29 August 1835.
4     L.A.O. T.d'E. H118/54, 3 September 1835 (*Letters A.T.*, I, p.141).
5     L.A.O. T.d'E. H116a/35, 28 September 1835; in his accompanying letter Charles added 'Frederick is a Pig.'
6     L.A.O. T.d'E. H119/49, 17 May 1836 (*Letters A.T.*, I, pp.142-43).
7     L.A.O. T.d'E. H119/50, n.d. [?May 1836].

in the old College Hall style with a screen, an oriel window, & the other windows mullioned in ancient fashion. There will be no ceiling but an oaken roof - & the fire place made for dogs. It will be like the hall of a manor house of yore....[1]

Charles was no amateur in these matters: he had been actively involved in advising his brother in law Matthew Russell over the furnishing of Brancepeth, and, following Matthew's death in 1822, supervised much of the remaining building work.[2] Like Brancepeth, Bayons was in the Gothic style, which appealed to his interests in the medieval past (and was seen by Charles as a tangible link with his d'Eyncourt forebears in the county). He first used his father's favoured architect, E. J. Willson of Lincoln, but soon tiring of his slowness, turned to another Lincoln architect, William Adams Nicholson (1803-1853), and, once more, to Anthony Salvin who was then working at Burwarton, the Shropshire home of Charles's niece Emma Hamilton. Salvin advised on architectural details, leaving most of the designs and the supervision of work on the site to Nicholson. The ideas, however were very much Charles's own. (His sons when resident in Lincolnshire and overseeing the work at Bayons received a constant stream of letters from their father full of detailed instructions.) Charles also drew on the advice of his friend Col. Thomas Wildman, whose own house, Newstead Abbey, Nottinghamshire, had been remodelled in the Gothic style in the 1820s.[3]

The foundations were laid in 1836. From then on, at his father's wish, Charles did not destroy but enclosed the old house in a carapace of extensions, variously described as 'Fake- or Sham- or Pseudo- or Operatic-Gothic'.[4] On 28 November 1836, Julia wrote to George Hildeyard, who had returned once more to Corfu:

All our brothers dropped off one by one after you left us - & now we are quite solitary & this place is growing daily more melancholy. This little book room is gradually darkening over us from the rising wall close to it & we begin to fancy ourselves some unfortunate nuns in the act of being bricked up - except that Potts' and Stark's faces occasionally grinning in at the window remind us that we are not quite under conventual regulations....[5]

Over the coming years, full details of the building work were relayed by the family to George Hildeyard. Clara wrote at length on 29 December 1836:

1    L.A.O. T.d'E. H116a/33, 29 August 1835.
2    For Charles's supervisory work at Brancepeth after Matthew's death see correspondence at L.A.O. 4T.d'E. H24-31.
3    For the building of Bayons see Tennyson & Dyson, pp.88-91; Mark Girouard, *The Victorian Country House*, rev. edn (London, 1979), pp.44-45, 103-09; *idem*, *The Return to Camelot* (London, 1981), pp.64-86; Terence R. Leach and Robert Pacey, *Lost Lincolnshire Country Houses. Volume 3. Bayons Manor, Tealby* (Burgh le Marsh, 1992). For Col. Wildman (1787-1859) see especially Rosalys Coope, 'The Wildman family, and Colonel Thomas Wildman of Newstead Abbey, Nottinghamshire', *Trans. Thoroton Soc.*, XCV (1991), pp.50-66. Also the account by J. Bernard Burke, 'extracted from his work, "The Visitation of Seats and Arms"' included in his *Memorials of Bayons Manor...*
4    *Letters A.T.*, I, xvii.
5    L.A.O. T.d'E. H119/102.

The building seems scarcely to have advanced since you left - being not yet covered in. The oriel is up but not the gable above it. The servants's hall is entirely slated & the dining hall as far as the room is finished - but we have had a tremendous storm of snow for the last week which has put an end to all farther proceedings for the present. The turret, which forms part of the old dining room, Papa has carried up into a tower which looks beautiful - giving the appearance of being octagonal - which has completed [sic] annihilated the bay look it possessed when you were here. He has projected a very high battlement upon the Westminster Hall corbels rendered double by the addition of corbels made of the Tealby stone, the color of the different stone agrees remarkably well - between the corbels large holes are left for the purpose of throwing rubbish &c upon the heads of the assailants, thus giving a fortified appearance to the tower, which far from overpowering the building gives both centre & mass - it is carried very little higher than the gable. The bay window to the north of the library is now up & is really magnificent. The old drawing & dining rooms are ready for slating. Papa has been particularly fortunate in his slate it being a very good color, it is Festiniogg, & has very much the appearance of lead. I like it better than any I have seen....[1]

A month later Eustace advised George Hildeyard, 'I understand the building at Bayons is going on very well and improves in beauty and grandeur by every stone & slate that is put upon it.... I think altogether that when finished it will be fit for the highest and richest nobleman in the land.'[2]

During the building work, the family left Bayons for Usselby. In April 1837, Ellen reported to George Hildeyard:

[W]e are at Usselby which looks very neat & cheerful after Tealby, & it is quite a treat to see the sun in the rooms. We have been here for a fortnight & intend to remain for the present.... Mr Nicholson promises us the 2 old rooms by July & they are getting on with them as fast as possible. The bed-rooms over them are splendid rooms, the old ceiling being taken away they are much higher; which additional height, makes them look much larger. Really the house is quite a palace (not "gew-gaw" however) now, that the north wing is nearly up. The deer also are now turned out & it is beautiful to see them graize on the hill to the north of the house....[3]

The strain and stress of all this work took its toll on Charles's health; as early as November 1836, Fanny advised George Hildeyard:

Your father has been very poorly, with a continued pain about the heart, and spasmodic pains in his limbs, arising from one and the same cause, a partial and slow circulation. The continual blunders and botheration, and vexation, attendant on the building harrasses and irritates him in so great a degree, as to produce a wish that it had never been begun. However I hope he will in the end be gratified, when it is completed, as it certainly will be very beautiful. Broadgates business has annoyed him not a litle....[4]

1  L.A.O. T.d'E. H119/113.
2  L.A.O. T.d'E. H121/6, 18 January 1837.
3  L.A.O. T.d'E. H121/29, 26 April 1837.
4  L.A.O. T.d'E. H119/103, 29 November 1836. Note also Charles Tennyson d'Eyncourt

Charles had been in dispute with John and Samuel Broadgate following their alleged assault on his stonemason, Tomline. The brothers were committed to prison but the affair was to cause embarrassment to Charles for some months to come. In January, John Broadgate advertised his release in the county press and thanked 'the *Seven Hundred Gentlemen* who voluntarily memorialized the Secretary of State for a remission of the sentence passed upon J.B. for a Breach of the Peace forced upon him by the unreasonable seizure and detention of his Tools and Implements at Bayons Manor'. The affair was no doubt in Fanny's mind when she wrote to George Hildegard on 26 February 1837, 'The building proceeds - the Lion (cut in stone by Tomline) supporting the shield, is erected over the porch, and very modestly underneath peeps *En avant*, which looks very well and presents a very nice appearance, altho' I fear it may call forth some animadversions from the envious & jealous, against whose darts there are no shields....'[1]

In April 1837 she reported that Charles was 'very low-spirited', continuing,

> but I hope it only arises from his anxiety about the building, in which his heart is now so entirely and exclusively engaged, as to preclude all other ideas, be they of what import they may, and as to parliament he says "I hate the very name of it." I am not surprised at his taking such great interest, in so beautiful an edifice as it every day shews itself more and more to be, and particularly when it will be a lasting memorial of taste and genius, and which is completely the work of his hands, in which few architects would have so completely excelled; but I often contemplate and tremble at the consequences that may hereafter ensue - for a large house demands every thing in proportion. I know your father would laugh at me, and has done so, when I have hastened to express the sentiments I now do to you....[2]

It was perhaps no surprise that within a few days Charles was attacked by what he called 'one of my old spasms. It did not produce insensibility - but has left me weak....'[3]

---

to George Hildeyard, 29 December 1833: 'I have not been well lately, but I am taking great care of myself. I have led a life of too much excitement. Late hours, contested election &c have nearly done me up. However I think I shall scramble over it. It is my *heart* which plagues me. I have too many things on my hands....' (L.A.O. T.d.'E H113/78). At the same time Louis informed George Hildeyard: 'My father, you will be sorry to learn, has been far from well for some time past. He suffers almost constantly from pain in his heart, & being very much harassed with cares and business is sometimes in a very nervous state. I think he might yet get well again, if he could dispose of his various business, were to leave parliament, & take to a quiet life in the country....' (L.A.O. T.d.'E H113/75).

1   *Lincoln, Rutland and Stamford Mercury*, 27 January 1837; L.A.O. T.d'E. H121/14. See also T. d'E. H121/8.

2   L.A.O. T.d'E. H121/30, 27 April 1837. See also Mrs Fanny Tennyson d'Eyncourt to George Hildeyard of 26 February 1837, '[Your father] has really at this present time, so much to excite, and annoy, in a variety of ways, that I frequently tremble for the consequences' (L.A.O. T.d.'E H121/14).

3   L.A.O. T.d'E. H120/42, 2 May 1837.

Victoria's accession in June 1837 once more revived Charles's hopes of a peerage. In September 1837 Fanny informed George Hildeyard of the recent speculation:

> As to the peerage we know nothing beyond what the papers announce. If true, I hope something worth having will accompany it. The house of Bayons or rather *palace* (as Mr. Bourne christens it) is progressing but not so as to ensure our speedy return - indeed I think it quite decided that we shall be obliged to remain the winter here....[1]

In March 1838 (the family were still at Usselby, but preparing to leave for the Coronation), Julia advised George Hildeyard,

> Tealby is growing tho' not very perceptibly. The only exterior part unfinished is the wall round the stable yard which will I think be a great feature. They are glazing the windows & putting in much painted glass. When we return from London we shall probably adjourn there. I believe Papa is still talked of as one of the *to be* Coronation Peers - but we hear nothing as he tells us *no news* in his letters.[2]

The visit to London coincided with the news that the anticipated peerage was not to be. William Russell once again canvassed Melbourne (now Prime Minister) on his Uncle's behalf, only to be informed that 'I should be wanting in fairness, if I did not say at once that I do not contemplate the possibility of my being able to include Mr Deyncourt.' Melbourne's reply was conveyed to Charles by Elizabeth Russell who was to add a characteristic response:

> I grieve while transcribing that cold-blooded reply. No doubt he is, & *will be* beset with aspiring applicants, still he might have written more courteously. Alas! man in ministerial shape slinks away from the remembrance of favours. His life is governed by selfish anticipations circumstances deadening his finer feelings. Who ever heard of gratitude flourishing in the atmosphere of courts! Some upstart who *has done nothing* may have a coronet before you or William because *something* may be *expected*. I am bitter, that is not right, but truth will come forth....

She also included her son's observation '... I am most certain there is no friendly feeling to my uncle on the part of ministers, still I do not see why we should give it up'.[3] Further petitions were submitted in 1839, in 1840 and in 1841, all without success - though Charles was offered, but presumably declined, the office of Provost Marshal General of Grenada for his son, George Hildeyard.[4]

---

Once they had returned from the Coronation festivities in London the d'Eyncourts were able to move back to Bayons and immerse themselves in Charles's vision - though this was understandably small consolation for the lack of a peerage. Over the coming years Charles ordered paintings, tapestries, armour (some bought at the

[1] L.A.O. T.d'E. H121/63, 26 September 1837.
[2] L.A.O. T.d'E. H122/67, 30 March 1837.
[3] L.A.O. T.d'E. H122/74, 12 April 1837.
[4] L.A.O. 2T.d'E. H35/42-49.

Eglinton Tournament sale in May 1840) and other furnishings appropriate to this 'Palace of Art'. He also began to transform Bayons into something akin to a castle, building an outer wall with an impressive gatehouse with drawbridge over the moat, and a large castellated inner wall (which included the kitchen range) to the north of the house with towers and gatehouses; a final touch (completed in 1842) was the construction of a ruined keep as part of the inner wall. Throughout, Charles's aim was to convey a sense of change through time. The ruined keep was designed as Early Norman and other parts were built in successive architectural styles - the analogy of course was with the imagined evolution of the ancient family of d'Eyncourt from the time of the Conquest onwards. The neighbours, with native Lincolnshire scepticism, dealt ruthlessly with all of Charles's pretensions; they particularly enjoyed repeating the butler's classic response to a visitor: 'The Right Honourable Gentleman is walking on the barbican.'[1]

——

Following their return from London in 1838, and although the work on the house was far from complete, the family began to entertain lavishly at Bayons. The most splendid of all events was the magnificent ball held there on 25 January 1842, an occasion reported at length in the county press:

> The Right Hon. C. T. d'Eyncourt gave a most splendid supper and ball on Tuesday evening last in honour of the Royal christening. The company, including several of his private friends, the neighbouring tradesmen and farmers, their wives, sons and daughters, exceeded 300 in number, a great proportion of whom commenced dancing in the spacious drawing-room, recently finished, about nine o'clock, and continued it with great spirit till the announcement of supper, which was served up in the noble banquetting-hall. The company, when seated, combined with the paintings, suits of armour, and other decorations of this noble apartment, presented one of the most splendid scenes, perhaps, ever witnessed in the private residence of a country gentleman. Towards the close of supper, Mr. d'Eyncourt gave successively the healths of the Queen, Prince Albert, and the Prince of Wales, introducing each by an appropriate speech; and to each a respond of nine hearty cheers was given, followed by appropriate airs from the band in the gallery, who had been playing during the progress of supper. Mr. d'Eyncourt then drank the healths of the company, stating the gratification himself and his lady felt at seeing them; after which, Z. Barton, Esq. proposed the healths of the worthy host and hostess, which were received by nine such cheers as made the mansion ring. Supper being over, dancing was resumed in the drawing-room until 7 o'clock, when the company retired to their homes, highly gratified with the urbanity and kindness of the host and worthy hostess, and the pleasure of an evening long to be remembered by all.[2]

Most of Charles's family were present, including Eustace, who had returned to Bayons in August 1841 from Gibraltar. He left on 30 January, sailing on 3 February

1  Martin, p.213.
2  *Lincoln, Rutland and Stamford Mercury*, 28 January 1842.

from Falmouth to join his regiment in Barbados. Just over a month later he was dead. George Hildeyard's diary entry for 13 April is a graphic one:

> Left Brocklesby with the afflicting news of poor Eustace's death at Barbadoes of yellow fever on the 8th March
> shocking                                                                                    arrived at B.M.
> shocking[1]

Charles Tennyson d'Eyncourt never fully recovered from this loss. Julia expressed the family's grief eloquently in some verses, "To My Dear Brother Eustace" (Appendix), written after Charles had placed a bell in a tower at Bayons to commemorate his son:

> I will not weep for thee
> I will not weep for thee
> For thy spirit is now
> Far more happy and free
> Than it could be below
> > My Brother.
>
> ...
>
> And to thy mem'ry sounds
> That bell thou can'st not hear
> And ev'ry hour it tolls
> Brings those to thee more near
> No other hope consoles
> > My Brother.[2]

------

Julia's verses survive in a copy kept by Edward Bulwer-Lytton (1803-1873). He represented Lincoln in Parliament from 1832 to 1841 and became a close friend of Charles's. George Hildeyard's diaries show the d'Eyncourts to have been regularly in Bulwer's company when in London and frequent visitors to Knebworth, his seat in Hertfordshire;[3] Bulwer paid visits to Bayons and much of his novel *Harold, the Last of the Saxons* (1848) - dedicated to Charles - was written in the Tapestry Room there. Bulwer was to be a player in another tragedy which deeply affected Charles.

Bulwer, who had been estranged from his wife since 1833, seems to have flirted with Julia who, in her innocence and inexperience, was captivated (tradition in the Tennyson family says that she fell deeply in love with him), but then

[1]  L.A.O. Misc. Don. 860/4.
[2]  H.R.O. D/EK C18/128. Compare Julia's poem with her cousin Charles Tennyson's "My Brother" in *Poems by Two Brothers* (Louth, 1827).
[3]  L.A.O. Misc. Don. 860. The tragedian William Macready's diaries also make passing reference to the friendship between Tennyson d'Eyncourt and Bulwer-Lytton; see Sir Frederick Pollock (ed.), *Macready's Reminiscences, and Selections from his Diaries and Letters*, 2 vols (London, 1875); William Toynbee (ed.), *The Diaries of William Charles Macready 1833-1851*, 2 vols (London, 1912). Tennyson d'Eyncourt and Alfred Tennyson were amongst the fifty stewards at Macready's farewell dinner, presided over by Bulwer-Lytton, on 1 March 1851.

withdrew, turning increasingly to religion. She wrote of her feelings to Bulwer in September 1845:

> Would that I had it in my power to pour the balm into your heart that you have poured into mine. Most bitterly have I lamented that in an unguarded moment of nervous excitement, I not only exposed that which, had I deserved all the praise you lavish upon me, should have been kept secret to the end of time, - but I have opened a source of pain & self-reproach to you, to which in all your generous sympathy for me, you almost forget to allude. At least, then let me endeavour to take out the sting of your suffering as you have done of mine. And first let me assure you that you need not ask my forgiveness - for my condemnation was ever directed against myself, not you - & if the sense of my own weakness was the cause of bitter remorse & humiliation, was it not also this, that, in bringing me to religion for my only solace & support, has been ultimately the source of real comfort & perhaps eternal benefit to me. Let this thought console, & assuage the pain I may have given you....[1]

Julia's religious fervour had been long-standing - she was known as 'The Saint' by the family and used a small oratory built in the grounds of Bayons - but when it was clear by early 1846 she was more than toying with conversion to Roman Catholicism, Charles reacted strongly. He had supported the Maynooth Grant in Parliament; like his father before him, was friendly with the Heneages of Hainton, a leading Catholic family in the county, and had for many years welcomed as a visitor to Bayons, James Simkiss (1771-1855), the Roman Catholic priest at Hainton. He was, however, far less tolerant of Catholicism when it came to his own family. Julia was sent to Cheltenham to stay with her Aunt Russell whilst plans were made to take her to Paris. She wrote to George Hildeyard from Cheltenham in May 1846 to inform him that the journey to Paris was postponed:

> I know the liberality of your nature & shall confide in it when I am allowed or driven to seek a refuge from the storm - but I hope at present things are settling. My father consents to the *freer* exercise of my religion provided I am cautious in not publishing *unnecessarily* my conversion a permission that amply satisfies me. Whether I am to go abroad, or to be allowed an entrance at Bayons - & indeed whether I should not prefer the former to the latter, depends on my father's disposition with regard to me.[2]

Charles, Julia and Clara finally left England for France in August 1846. It was first planned that Julia would enter a convent at Boulogne, but the party travelled on to Paris leaving Julia with friends - she subsequently entered the Congregation du Notre Dame at nearby Conflans and later the convent at Chaillot. Charles and Clara then visited Aincourt, where he negotiated to buy the chateau, in the hope that Julia would live there with a companion (an idea finally abandoned in 1847). Julia arrived at Bayons in January 1847 but returned to France in September and by November once more had entered the convent at Conflans. Her father fetched her from France in March 1848. In May she moved to the guest house of St Mary's Convent at Princethorpe near Rugby. The event which Charles feared the most (and to which he

1   H.R.O. D/EK C/145, 4 September 1845.
2   L.A.O. T.d'E. H130/13, n.d. [?May 1846].

responded with great anger) occurred in 1850, when Julia entered the novitiate, taking her final vows in 1852. She remained at Princethorpe until her death in 1879.[1]

---

It was probably towards the end of the 1840s that Charles started to write an elegy in three Cantos to his son Eustace.[2] Although overtly writing about Eustace, his favourite son, it is likely that Charles was also mourning the loss of Julia, his favourite daughter. The first Canto begins with a picturesque account of Eustace's childhood and a description of his deathbed; the second recreates the banquet of January 1842 which marked both the christening of the infant Prince of Wales and Eustace's departure for the West Indies. D'Eyncourt introduces a strange episode in which an Ancient Mariner-like interloper with 'brilliant eye' holds the company spellbound while he recounts the growth of the monarchy from the days of Edward III. The interloper turns out to be Eustace in disguise - an unintentionally ironic comment on the artificial creation of a Family History by the newly sprung d'Eyncourts. The poem's heart, structurally and emotionally, is the interchange between father and son in which a golden chalice is exchanged as a token of their love. Only in the third canto does the over-weening ambition of the writer move from the touchingly amateurish to the artistically pretentious, with an embarrassing attempt at philosophy in the style of Pope's *Essay on Man*, revealing the inevitable triteness of the expression of genuine, and no doubt deep, emotion by a writer of no talent. Charles had remained utterly untouched by the Romantic period: he was still the worthy schoolboy of the 1790s, reciting heroic couplets as for a school speech-day.

The first mention of the poem comes in a letter from Elizabeth Russell writing from Cheltenham on 17 July 1849:

> I looked in the back drawing room for your poem, & felt an unwarrantable disappointment; only some small lopping of redundancies seem advisable, to add to its beauty is not in my power, "small blame" to me for that.[3]

In June 1850, Alfred Tennyson's *In Memoriam A.H.H.* was issued. This led to encouragement from Charles's family to publish his own verses. Clara wrote to her father on 6 June 1850:

> "A prophet was never without honour save in his own country &c". Print your poem by all means. Forster must be a very good judge, tho' he does admire Alfred Tennyson's verses, at any rate, he evidently sides with the popular

---

1   For Julia in these years see especially L.A.O. T.d'E. H132, 134 & 135. Charles's health was, once more, under great strain. He wrote to George Hildeyard on 22 July 1848, 'I was taken very ill in the House last night with one of my worst spasms & to day feel not equal to the least exertion, having been under its influence for 2 hours altho' I did not faint - I could not stay the division' (L.A.O. T.d'E. H131/26).

2   Perhaps Charles was spurred on by the appearance in 1847 of *The Princess*, his nephew's first volume for five years. Ellen wrote to her father on 31 December 1847, 'Alfred Tennyson's new poem called "The Princess" is just published - but Emma [Hamilton] says it contains but little beauty' (L.A.O. 2 T.d'E. H44/1).

3   L.A.O. 2T.d'E. H52/20.

taste....[1]

Elizabeth Russell similarly enjoined her brother to publish in a letter dated a week later: 'When are your Cantos to be printed? Let us shew on *this* side of our House "We are Poets"!'[2] Louis soon added his thoughts, 'I liked the Poem very much - the alterations you have made within the last year have improved it amazingly - and there is no monotony in it - which I imagine is very difficult to avoid in that kind of rhyme...'[3]

Bulwer's friend John Forster (1812-1876), having been canvassed for his opinion, finally offered his criticism on 9 July:

> Your poem is very badly "pointed". The superabundance of dashes is quite uncalled for, and, besides being a hideous disfigurement of the page, not seldom obscures the sense. I began to correct them - but they were so numerous that I was obliged to stop at the second page. Pray strike them out remorselessly - you will not seldom find a mere comma the best substitute for them.
>
> I retain my opinion generally of the poem - & have marked some doubtful rhymes - and one or two hasty suggestions - which may, or may not, be worth attending to. They are not of any importance in reference to the entire poem.[4]

To judge from the retention of the dashes in the published version, Charles chose to ignore Forster's advice but this does not seem to have affected Forster's loyalty. On 24 September, writing from Knebworth, he once more addressed Charles:

> I saw the "Elegy" here a few weeks back, & would have written to ask why you did not send me a copy but that I heard from Bulwer of some changes you were making in the drawings. I claim a copy when you can let me have it.[5]

William Davy & Son, Charles's printers, were ready 'to complete the poem' in November,[6] but publication was to be delayed to the following year. From December 1850 to February 1851, there was much discussion in the family about the lithographs - Charles certainly did not approve of their original 'coffee colour'.[7] But of greater concern was the dedication. Charles once more returned to his (and his brother's) Muse, Elizabeth Russell (whose son William had died earlier in the year). She wrote to her brother from Brancepeth on 16 December 1850:

> [I]s it adviseable to dedicate your poem to me, having a sister who might deem herself offended by the preference? She is, I *know*, considered the one of your heart & may at present, as formerly, so consider herself. Of this *I ask not*. There is among the *mysteries* of our *being* something like mesmeric influence & we are (I think) scarcely responsible for our *taste* & *distaste* of individuals. Now

[1]  L.A.O. 2T.d'E. H51a/24.
[2]  L.A.O. 2T.d'E. H51a/25, 13 June 1850.
[3]  L.A.O. T.d'E. H44/21, 4 July 1850.
[4]  L.A.O. T.d'E. H135/24; also L.A.O. 2T.d'E. H55/17, Forster to d'Eyncourt, 4 July 1850.
[5]  L.A.O. T.d'E. H160/22.
[6]  L.A.O. 2T.d'E. H54/29, 19 November 1850.
[7]  L.A.O. 2T.d'E. H55/25, 5 December 1850. For Elizabeth Russell and her daughter Emma's comments on the lithographs see L.A.O. T.d.'E. H136/2-3.

dearest Charley, don't for *one instant* imagine, while writing thus, that a morbid inclination to question your affection is indulged. There is a life in your pen which must proceed from the life of your heart, but I would have you avoid exciting jealousy.... I admire the dedication & it touches me to feel that my name might be perpetuated with that sweet angelic creature's. As to residence, it would be *much* better, *much more simple* to omit any, besides, no longer of Brancepeth, or of Hardwicke (for poor William let the last unknown to me, *on lease*) *neither* ought to appear & *Cheltenham* sounds, *as it is, vulgar* · *Mrs*, also, disagreeably so. Those added lines, I fancy, only few would comprehend, the *subject* incomprehensible, & few in the railway days have licence to attend to more than their *material* carpet-bags, but the soliloquy is wonderfully executed upon a subject beyond the reach of human wings. The Christianity is also well-managed....

She added one further comment as to the text: 'When 3 lines rhyme I like a bracket comme ça } is it too old fashonn'd? [*sic*][1] Her daughter Emma, wrote on 20 December, 'My Mother is willing to accept the dedication, & hopes you will not in any way alter the wording of it. We *prefer* Elizabeth Russell & that no residence should be named.'[2] *Eustace; an Elegy* was issued in the early spring of 1851, some nine months after his nephew's *In Memoriam* which had received instant acclaim.

Charles himself was hopeful of some popular acclaim. In a letter to George Hildeyard of July 1851 he confidently anticipated that it would 'be reviewed in the Globe, Sun & Athenaeum and its appearance in the New Monthly will give a more personal character to the review of it'.[3] In this Charles was to be frustrated: *Eustace* was not printed in the *New Monthly*.[4] He was further advised by H. Porter Smith, who had sent a copy to Ainsworth, editor of the *New Monthly*, and was willing to send another

to 'an influential' friend of mine on the "Times" and ask him to oblige me with a notice - at the same time you must hold me harmless of any thing that wilful paper may say or do - they are as likely to indulge their feelings towards you as a public man as to do justice to your parental sorrows or poetic powers - and my friend tho' he may procure the insertion of the criticism will not write it.

*You* must judge - depend on it I will do my best - but that paper is a wild animal that wounds even its keepers to appear ruthless & independent.[5]

Reaction in the family and among friends is less easy to follow. George Hildeyard's diaries make no mention of it[6] and there are likewise few references to it in the family correspondence. Considering the general loquacity of the family on all

---

1    L.A.O. T.d'E. H135/35. Elizabeth Russell's reference to her sister, Mrs Bourne, may have reflected her knowledge that Mr Bourne was dying (his death took place at Cleethorpes on 15 December 1850).
2    L.A.O. T.d'E. H163/22.
3    L.A.O. T.d'E. H136/40, 14 July 1851.
4    See however a brief review in *The New Monthly Magazine and Humorist*, 92 (August 1851), p.483.
5    L.A.O. T.d'E. H136/72, 13 August 1851.
6    L.A.O. Misc. Don. 860/9 & 10 (diaries for 1850 & 1851).

subjects, their silence might suggest a certain embarrassment. Charles's old friend Col. Wildman was however unreservedly enthusiastic when he wrote to George Hildeyard on 29 September:

> I cannot tell you how delighted I am with your father's Elegy... I knew him to be *talented* beyond the common range; but had no idea of his powers as a Poet. The subject, no doubt, gave energy and permanence to his Genius - but the genius slumbering there is indeed of no common order - I have read nothing *at all equal* to it *as a poem*, since the days of Byron.[1]

A review in the *Gentleman's Magazine* for November 1851 more ambiguously observed 'The circumstances of such a publication disarm criticism: nor do the verses require any apology for their sentiment or expression, which are alike far above mediocrity. Such effusions are sacred; and if we would take any exception, it is merely to ask, why should such a publication be *published* at all? as, no doubt, its circulation is eventually, with scarcely an exception, private and gratuitous.' The reviewer, however questioned d'Eyncourt's handling of the historical evidence relating to Edward of Woodstock's 'Triple Plume of purest white' (Canto II, note 2), which was also prominent on the binding: 'To quote an historical antiquary in corroboration of a popular error which he has done his best to refute, is surely the "unkindest cut of all."'[2] This stung Elizabeth Russell to write to Charles:

> *Nasty* Mr Sylvanus *Urban*, I suppose that means in the *shade*. I hope he is well trimmed - everyone here admires Eustace.

She continued, 'I was thinking last night, while on your pillow, that if it had been bound in black with an urn upon it, *some* might have thought it even a more appropriate gift *to a mourner*'.[3]

The simple truth was that hinted at by the *Gentleman's Magazine* reviewer: *Eustace* (unlike Alfred's *In Memoriam*) was only destined to have a very limited circulation. Although a second edition was called for, most of the copies (250 of the first edition and fifty of the second) were bound up in J. B. Burke's *Memorials of Bayons Manor...* issued in 1852.[4] *Eustace* remains very much a minor work in the eighteenth-century tradition which by its very smallness sets off the greatness of Alfred Tennyson's achievement in *In Memoriam*. Charles Tennyson d'Eyncourt's memorial was to be in the architecture of Bayons Manor rather than in verse. Perhaps the final word should be Alfred's only recorded comment (made in 1883): 'It

---

[1]  L.A.O. T.d'E. H136/80. Also Wildman to George Hildeyard of 7 October 1851: 'I wrote to you exactly what I thought of the Elegy. It is a highly finish'd beautiful work. I am very fastidious as to Poetry and my title of Poet. Every school-boy can write verses - and most well educated men can put their ideas into metre. Rogers ("Melodious Rogers") is certainly worthy of a niche. But most of the others you mention are *equivocal*, and must I fear, *travel 2nd class*. I have read your cousin *lately*, and with much pleasure - there are frequent flashes of genius - but he takes more liberties in *affectation of wildness* than his reputation will justify' (L.A.O. T.d.'E H136/83).

[2]  *Gentleman's Magazine* (December 1851), p.527.

[3]  L.A.O. T.d'E. H134/35, 9 November 1851.

[4]  L.A.O. T.d'E. H138/30, J. B. Burke to Tennyson D'Eyncourt, 4 June 1852.

was written by an uncle of mine who fancied himself a Poet and was - a considerable humbug.'[1]

Alfred's success continued to goad his uncle's family. Following the publication of "The Charge of the Light Brigade" in December 1854, Marianne Hutton wrote to George Hildeyard, 'I *do* wish your Father would exercise his truly elegant pen on a subject so well adapted to his gifted mind! and Alfred Tennyson might then hide his diminished head.'[2] Charles's response is not recorded, but to judge from the events two months later, he held his (increasingly successful) nephew in low regard. *Fraser's Magazine* for February 1855 contained an anonymous article 'A week in the Wolds of Lincolnshire', which made a clear contrast between Bayons 'a mansion which may hold its own with the most princely of our princely countryhouses' with the humble village parsonage in which the author assumed Alfred Tennyson to have been born.[3] Charles commented to George Hildeyard, 'As to Alfred's boyhood at Tealby, it is not true. He was a Somersbyite altogether.' He continued (echoing his comment of 1833),

> What rubbish that is which you quote from memory as part of his last production! What a strange thing that such a writer should be so generally admired & covered with laurels by the Queen! Perhaps it is our want of taste which blinds us to his merits![4]

Less than a week later he again returned to his attack (of "The Charge of the Light Brigade"):

> ... The verses also I thank you for - not for *their own merit*! but on account of the trouble you have kindly taken to procure them. Horrid rubbish indeed! What a discredit it is that British taste & Poetry should have such a representative before the Nations of the Earth & Posterity! for a Laureate will so appear. Posterity will, it is hoped, have a sound judgement on such matters, & if so what an Age this must appear when such trash can be tolerated & not only tolerated but enthusiastically admired!! However I do not wish to have my opinion circulated as to my nephew's talents - for it would only appear to many that I am either without taste or spiteful, & he hearing of it would deem it ungracious &c.[5]

Charles's subsequent opinions on his nephew are not recorded (the rich family correspondence which survived from the earlier years at this point begins to peter out). One can only speculate on his response to *Maud*, published in the same year,

---

1    E. A. Horsman (ed.), *The Diary of Alfred Domett 1872-1885* (Oxford, 1953), p.272. Domett adds 'He was the younger son and got the estate which ought to have been his (T's) father's. "And when Hallam (the historian) heard of it" added Tennyson laughing, he exclaimed "The d——d scoundrel - then he has got the name and the money too!"' (pp.272-73).

2    L.A.O. T.d'E. H163/53, n.d. [?December 1854].

3    [?Philip Pusey], 'A week in the Wolds of Lincolnshire', *Fraser's Magazine*, LI (February 1855), pp.173-81.

4    L.A.O. T.d'E. H141/10, 6 February 1855.

5    L.A.O. T.d'E. H141/13, 11 February 1855.

with its references to the 'gewgaw castle', the hated grandfather and the hero's enemy, 'lord of the broad estate and the hall'.

———

Charles lost his seat at Lambeth in the election of July 1852. Bulwer wrote to him as soon as he had heard the result:

> I cannot tell you how grieved I am at the loss of your election It has thrown a damp over my spirits which is most depressing. Those vulgar electors with their low idea of public men! You who were such a credit and honour to them! But perhaps you will be much happier free... the loss of an election, may be no great sorrow.[1]

Although Charles retained an interest in politics, he withdrew more and more into private life and into his vision of the ancient past of his family, spending much time at his chateau at Aincourt.

Weston Cracroft of Hackthorn was an occasional visitor to Bayons during these years. In January 1857, he found his host, still very much engaged in county politics, 'a wonderfully hale man for 73'; he noted further, 'Mr D'Eyncourt has some good talk, tho a bit of a quack, even trying out to make himself a great man.' His comments on Bayons are telling:

> Whoever would think for all the pomp and circumstance and pretended ancestry of Bayons Manor that its owner was the son of my grandfather's attorney at Market Rasen? Beautifully done in every respect as is Bayons it is the ridicule of the County.
>
> ... I was walking about Bayons Manor with its sham keep and drawbridge and moat, and thought what an exquisite piece of tomfoolery it is - but still an enchanting pretty situation.

D'Eyncourt took him to see his latest project, the village school, 'which Mr D'Eyncourt is building at his sole expense'. Cracroft continued:

> It is very handsome. The outside is completed.... The interior is by no means completed but promises to be quite equal if not superior to the exterior. The roof internally is made entirely of Mr D'Eyncourt's timber - Scotch fir - poplar - and the whole has been done by village workmen, Mr D'E sole architect.[2]

Charles had modelled the interior on Westminster Hall. This was not the last of Charles's antiquarian projects. Various county families had made gifts of stained-glass windows to Lincoln cathedral, and, not to be outdone, in 1858 Charles presented a cinquefoil window to the cathedral in commemoration of its founder, Bishop Remigius - it was typical of d'Eyncourt that he was effectively commemorating Remigius's cousin, Walter d'Eyncourt, and thus his (Charles's) claimed family origins in Lincolnshire.[3]

———

[1] L.A.O. T.d'E. H160/35, n.d. [July 1852].
[2] Sir Francis Hill, 'The Cracroft diary', *T.R.B.* 3, 1 (1977), pp.26-29.
[3] *Illustrated London News*, 8 January 1859, p.28 (preceded, pp.27-28, by an account of Bayons and the d'Eyncourt family). Peter B. G. Binnall, *The Nineteenth Century Stained Glass in Lincoln Minster* (Lincoln, 1966).

Throughout these years Charles's friendship with Bulwer remained firm. In September 1859, having returned from a visit to Aincourt, Charles wrote to inform him, 'I found here your honoured chair! Did I not contact you to withhold it? I shall not like Knebworth so well when I see you sitting in any other - yet I *am gratified, deeply gratified* by this additional mark of your constant and unfailing friendship.... I have placed it in your own room which is immortalized by your pen, & it is regarded with great interest by our visitors.'[1] A few weeks later he commented 'I should like to see you installed in your chair and Tapestry Chamber where we would keep you quiet...'; he also thanked Bulwer for his 'expression of satisfaction at my reconciliation with my son the Captain'[2] (in another family upset, Charles had publicly disowned Edwin in January 1855). On 30 April 1861 he wrote to Bulwer:

> I have been seriously ill for 3 months, having been subject at the beginning of February, with what they tell me were the consequences of extreme mental fatigue which I had incurred by having got up & delivered within 3 preceding weeks, 4 long & elaborate *Astronomical Lectures*. It was absurd that I should have undertaken so much but I think I am now approaching a complete recovery - altho' it has required 3 months to accomplish such a result. I trust I may be able to go to London in the month of May & one of my greatest pleasures there will be to meet there one whose affectionate and constant kindness is one of the *very few* grounds of my remaining attachment to a continued existence.[3]

Was it at this time when, driving through the park at Bayons, he looked back at his lifetime's creation and murmured, 'I must have been mad!'?[4]

Charles died at the home of his daughter, Clara Hinde Palmer, in London on 21 July. His funeral, like that of his father, was a grand affair (though unlike the events of 1835, one member of his brother's family, Charles Turner, the vicar of Grasby, did attend). One of the local newpapers reported, 'The flag was drooping half-mast high on the tower of the beautiful house, that poem in stone, which his genius has left....'[5] Just over a century later, in October 1964, a demolition team 'in a sad flash of dynamite'[6] reduced Charles's Palace of Art to rubble.

If, however, an epitaph is needed for Bayons, and the hold the medieval dream had on ambitious, worldly, men in the 1830s, it can be found in the 'Dedicatory Epistle' of Bulwer-Lytton's *Harold*:

> [M]y thoughts naturally fly back to the associations I connected with your name when I placed it at the head of this epistle. Again I seem to find myself under your friendly roof; again to greet my provident host entering that gothic chamber in which I had been permitted to establish my unsocial study, heralding the advent of majestic folios, and heaping libraries round the unworthy work. Again, pausing from my labour, I look through that castle

1     H.R.O. D/EK C18/125, 30 September 1859.
2     H.R.O. D/EK C18/126, 19 October 1859.
3     H.R.O. D/EK C18/127, 30 April 1861.
4     Tennyson & Dyson, p.91.
5     *Market Rasen Weekly Mail*, 3 August 1861.
6     Martin, p.210.

casement, and beyond that feudal moat, over the broad landscapes, which, if I err not, took their name from the proud brother of the Conqueror himself: or when, in those winter nights, the grim old tapestry waved in the dim recesses, I hear again the Saxon thegn winding his horn at the turret door, and demanding admittance to the halls from which the prelate of Bayeux had so unrighteously expelled him.... With all those folios, giants of the gone world, rising around me daily, more and more, higher and higher - Ossa upon Pelion - on chair and table, hearth and floor... with all those disburied spectres rampant in the chamber, all the armour rusting in thy galleries, all those mutilated statues of early English kings... niched into thy grey, ivied walls - say in thy conscience, O host, ... shall I ever return to the nineteenth century again?[1]

---

[1]  *Harold, the Last of the Saxons*, 3 vols (London, 1848), I, xvii-xix. Bulwer wrote to Forster on 25 July 1861, 'I have been deeply grieved at D'Eyncourt's death' to which his friend replied on 27 July, 'Yes - poor D'Eyncourt's death was also a great regret to me, conveying me back to those old times in which you had that large share of my life and thoughts....' (H.R.O. D/EK C 27, letters 1855-61; D/EK C 14, unnumbered letter).

Figure 6: Bayons Manor and Park.
Lithograph by Dickinson and Co. for the frontispiece of Charles Tennyson d'Eyncourt's *Eustace* (1851). The original bears an inscription from Canto I: 'In those Woods and Groves, on Wold and Plain, / He dreamt of Life and Love, and dreamt in Vain!'

# POEMS BY GEORGE CLAYTON TENNYSON

George Clayton Tennyson's poems have received some attention, thanks to Sir Charles Tennyson's research, but they have never before been collected. In this edition our aim is to present a clean, reading text. "The Wandering Jew" and "It is the lot of man" pose the greatest editorial problems. Neither can be considered 'finished': there are many drafts of the stanzas and George continued to make alterations to his 'final' version which may, or may not, have been adopted. Our text of these two poems therefore presents George's first, coherent, finished version of the stanzas: with one or two exceptions, none of George's cancellations and emendations have been included. George's handwriting varies considerably, but we are satisfied that all the poems and fragments presented are in his hand and are his compositions.

## I. POEMS AND FRAGMENTS FROM G. C. TENNYSON'S COMMONPLACE BOOK[1]

*A Tribute to the Memory of Mr. Leander —— who drowned himself from despair of obtaining the love of Mrs —— of Wapping*

Clear was the night, the stars shone bright
The moon its silvery radiance shed
O'er mountain tree, and sky and sea
And every breeze, was hushed to peace
When pale Leander left his bed.

The sea to view, was clear and blue
And gentle riplings kissed the shore
Then from the steep, into the deep
With headlong spring he plunged in
And ne'er was seen or heard of more.

Yet oft the *mar*-iner from far
When bounding o'er the Northern Sea
On moonlight night, has heard his sprite
E'er and anon, with piteous moan
Howl *Osyter Man* O misery!

[p.56]. *c.*1807 (included in the early 'Directions for Bookbinding').

---

[1]    T.R.C. N 15.

# POEMS BY TWO BROTHERS

*A Sublime Ode in Two Parts on Wintry Weather*
*with moral inferences in imitation of that delectable and heaven born author and poet Mr.*
*Hervey; concluding with a sublime address to young and old, dames and misses, misers and*
*youths just breeched, and lastly to complete the climax to the illustrious sovereign who now*
*sways the sceptre of these realms, King George the third; in which in a method of deriving*
*consolation for the follies and excentricities of the heir apparent is humbly submitted to the*
*royal ear; the whole concluding with the most beautiful and sublime similes that have ever*
*met the eye of a candid and judicious public.*

### Part I
#### 1
'Tis a cold and dreary night in
Bleak December and the clear air
Bitter is and finger biting
Careless mortals then beware.

#### 2
Death is very keen and bitter
Dreary is the grave and cold
Cleave not to the world's vain glitter
All that glitters is not gold.

#### 3
Rivers bound by winter fast in
Icy chains forget to move
Mortals bound by views not lasting
Of true joys forgetful prove.

#### 4
Many youths on smooth ice sliding
Venture from the safer shore,
Till the treacherous glass dividing
In they plunge to rise no more.

#### 5
Youths let none not tried be trusted
Villains smile to gain their end
Few are not with vice encrusted
Trust not all who call you friend.

#### 6
Icicles in moon beam glister
Gently falls the dazzling snow
We are all deceived, good Mister
By the tinsel of below.

64

### 7

Vain the world and noise and trouble
Gilded pill and glittering show
Life itself is but a bubble
Frail as ice and light as snow.

### 8

Fleecy flakes of pearly lustre
Are but splendid for a day
Check fond Man thy pride and bluster
Soon thyself shall turn to clay.

### 9

Yet as snow dissolved to water
Puddly splash, or drizzly rain
Still may shine as snow hereafter
When exhaled by heat again.

### 10

So o'er will and sin victorious
Free from rottenness and worm
Shall we rise in triumph glorious
In a new and radiant form.

### 11

Howls the gale thro' unclasped window
Leaves are scattered in the blast
Emblem sure of us who sin do
So 'twould be with us at last.

### 12

Yet the leaves revive shall never
Man shall flourish in the skies
They shall fall to fall for ever
We shall fall again to rise.

### 13

Cold it is, but coalfire blazes
Thus Religion cheers the mind
Sin benumbed thy heart it raises
Where substantial joys thoul't find.

### 14

Mortal proud, yet void of reason
Take th'instruction of a friend
Ponder well the wintry season
And thoul't prosper in thy end.

### Part II
### 15

On a broomstick or a fiddle
Harvey prates, why should not I
Prate of winter, now i'th' middle
Is it worse to prate than lye?

### 16

From all subjects grave deductions
Rise in good and pious mind
Greasy thus or sour eructions
Rise in throat from pent up wind.

### 17

From each theme 'tis Poet's glory
To derive some moral good
Tho' as foreign be the story
As King George from Old King Lud.

### 18

Young and old, robust and feeble
Learn to moralize apace
Ye whose base is turned to treble
Ye whose squeak is not yet base.

### 19

Dames desert your pins and laces
Ribbands, kerchiefs, caps and rings
And deduce sententious phrases
E'en from mean and trivial things.

### 20

Girls, desert your childish gew gaws
Baby houses, dolls and frocks
Hearken to my weighty new saws
Moralize, nor care who mocks.

21

Men who dream, of fame or riches
Ponder well the things I say
Youths, who just are cloath'd in breeches
Spurn your tops, nor heed your play.

22

Thou enthron'd in earthly splendor
George with Charlotte by thy side
Who, of Faith august Defender
Rul'st o'r nations far and wide.

23

Prince, with regal robe invested
Hearken to my moral lay
Then of earthly power divested
Thou shalt reign in endless day.

24

What tho' giddy sons perplex thee
Shake their elbows drink and wh—
What tho' wanton Jersey vex thee
Veteran Fitzherbert more.

25

What tho' of his wife and daughter
England's hope forgetful prove
And by base contrivance sought her
Life, who ought to be his love.

26

What tho' Brunswick's issue ducal
Be neglected and reviled
And thy son, to make us puke all
Wish'd to bastardize his child.

27

What tho' still the jaundiced Charlotte
Stimulate her impious son
Yet to stigmatize as harlot
One as spotless as the sun.

28

What tho' he in tricks detected
From Newmarket was kick'd off
And unworthily rejected
E'en of fools and knaves the scoff.

29

Yet come quickly, learn my science
And tho' he be mad and vile
Thou to grief shall bid defiance
And midst woes look up and smile.

30

Then thy breast shall know true comfort
Now th'abode of pain and care
Thus from smoke th'immortal Rumford
Clears contaminated air.

31

Thus dank mist and lowering vapour
Are dispelled by radiant light
Thus the beam of farthing taper
Dissipates the gloom of night.

32

Thus the traveller benighted
Wanders reckless of his way
Till by Venus he is lighted
Beauteous star with silvery ray.

33

Thus when pinched with want of dinner
Every visage wears a frown
Sirloin enters, every sinner
Smiles with glee, and gulps it down.

34

Thus fond youth, ill starred Leander
Thou didst brave the boisterous main
Wealthy Hero to Philander
Hero, meed of all thy pain.

### 35

And by waves and wild winds thwarted
Thou would'st view love's hallowed fire
Which like spark electric darted
Thro' thy nerves, did strength inspire.

### 36

[Luckless he who trusts in Woman
For the faithless lamp decay'd
Warn'd by me, henceforth let no man
Trust in widow wife or maid.][1]

[pp.62-71]. *c*.1806. Entered in the Contents, p.716, as 'A Sublime Ode in two parts on Wintry Weather'. Stanzas 18 to 29 and 15 to 29 respectively printed in 'Alfred's father', pp.287-89 and Tennyson & Dyson, pp.50-52, who observe: 'These relate to the doings of the Prince of Wales (afterwards George IV) and were no doubt written about 1805-6 when the first commission of inquiry into the conduct of his wife had been instituted, and the Prince, supported in some degree by his mother, was disputing with the King (George III) regarding the education of his unfortunate daughter and doing his best to have her removed from the state and public dignity which should have been accorded to his heiress-apparent.' George's reference in the title to 'that delectable and heaven born author and poet' is problematical. He may have been imitating the Revd James Hervey (1714-1758) whose *Meditations and Contemplations* (London, 1747) included a 'Winter Piece'. The vigorous style, however, suggests John, Baron Hervey, of Ickworth (1696-1743), noted both as a writer of prose and poetry.

*Verses Addressed to a Lady on her Departure.*

### 1

O I have passed a southern summer's day
The dazzling landscape dim'd th'astonish'd sight
And in that overpowering blaze of light
Entranc'd and lost I lay.

### 2

The sun is set, and indistinctly seen
The fading visions wear a graver hue
And softer prospects open to the view
Less vivid, more serene.

### 3

Yes from the memory of enjoyment past
A calm yet mingled pleasure[2] we derive
Mournful tho' sweet, which in our hearts alive
Shall ever, ever last.

---

1  George uses square brackets here.
2  Subsequently altered to 'feeling'.

4

And who this pensive pleasure would resign
This silent, tender luxury of thought
For all the unideal transports bought
By revelry and wine.

5

Imagination fades, enjoyments pall
But memory's pleasures never shall decay
Shall shine tho' clouds of age obscure our day
Shall bloom tho' vigour fail.

6

Can I forget thee? While the purple tide
That warms this heart, shall bid its pulse to play
That pulse shall beat for thee tho' far away
For thee and none beside.

7

Can I forget thee? In the festive hall
Where wit and beauty reign and minstrelsey
My heart still fondly shall recur to thee
Thy image still recal.

8

Can I forget thee? in the gloomy hour
When wave o'er wave, tempestuous passions roll
Thy lov'd idea still shall sooth my soul
And health and peace restore.

9

Farewell - may choicest blessings round thee wait
And kindred angels guard that angel's form
Guide and protect thee in life's ruder storm
And every blast of fate.

10

Star of the North farewell - thy brilliant ray
Shall happier skies illumine - O restore
To us thy lustre, visit us once more
Our life, our light, our day.

[p.295]. *c*.1807. Stanzas 7 to 9 printed (with several errors of transcription) in *Memoir*, I, p.11; printed in full in Tennyson & Dyson, pp.45-47, where it is said, 'Nothing is known about the lady to whom the poem is said to be addressed.' The lady, George's 'Star of the North', is almost certainly Elizabeth Russell. A later (mid to late 1820s), nine-stanza version is at L.A.O. T.d'E. H152/2. In this copy addressed to 'Miss Julia Tennyson / with the author's best compliments and respects', Stanza 3 is omitted and replaced with Stanza 5; stanza 7 (6), line 3 replaces 'My heart' with 'This heart'; the first line of Stanza 9 (8) reads 'May choicest gifts of heaven around thee wait'.

### [*Thy Monstrous Ears*]

#### 1

"Thy monstrous ears peep thro' thy borrow'd vest
Where didst thou steal that shaggy lyon's hide?
The royal beast to thee is nought allied
Thou art an ass at best.

#### 2

Thy cloven feet the knavery proclaim
The mangled melody of roar and bray
The notes unnatural at once betray
Thy nature and thy name.

#### 3

Restore vain daw the colours not thine own
The painted plumes which decorate thy tail
The lustre fled say what will then avail
That sooty hue alone?"

#### 4

O midnight these the sounds thy tongue convey'd
That iron tongue when erst at eventide
The muse in sweet yet mournful measures sigh'd
In plaintive numbers play'd.

#### 5

Astonish'd stood the bard; his fane was wreck'd
Flush'd his pale cheek with anger scarce repress'd
When thus the sable goddess he address'd
In innocence erect.

#### 6

"O thou lone power whose ebon throne inlaid
With living sapphire, burns; whose awful brow
The gems of heaven adorn, what time below
The earth is wrapt in shade.

71

7

Enjoy thy dreary pomp, yet why aspire
With envious mists to dim the solar rays
Still shall the radiant orb arise and blaze
With more refulgent fire.

8

Tho' faint eclipse may veil thy placid light
O moon awhile; anon thy silvery sphere
Emergent shall in silent glory cheer
The gloomy vault of night.

9

Thus from aspersion clear'd the poet's fame
Shall brightly shine; O midnight with disdain
The bard repels thy charge; a borrow'd strain
He proudly will disclaim.

10

In vain for him would nature then unfold
Her peerless treasures, should he fondly pore
Upon some antique song, and for rude ore
Exchange his sterling gold.

11

The generous lyon scorns the plunder'd prey
On native pinions borne, the bird of Jove
High towering soars into the realms above
And cleaves the fields of day.

12

Then shall the poet with ignoble art
Adopt some ancient and forgotten lay,
When to the flash of heaven, the taper's ray
Shall brilliance impart.

13

Yet how should he pursue the lofty strain
And weave poetic forms in fancy's loom
How cull from every flower the brightest bloom?
Alas! th'attempt is vain.

### 14

For they are lost who bade the minstrel sweep
The breathing chords of his devoted lyre
And irresponsive to its master's fire
The harp but wakes to weep."

*The Minstrel's Lament.*

### 15

Sweet is their memory as the dying close
Of musick heard afar; soft as the breeze
Which faintly whispers thro' the slumb'ring trees
In twilight's calm repose.

### 16

Sweet as the bells upon the varying gale
When mellow'd by the wave; soft as the tear
Which melts in beauty's eye, at sorrow's prayer
And flows at pity's tale.

### 17

Sweet as the perfume of the fading rose;
Soft as the moon reflected from the deep
In eve autumnal when the waters sleep
And not a zephyr blows.

### 18

Sweet and yet mournful as thy varied song
Sole chantress of the night; thy warblings clear
Steal with delicious languor on the ear
The listening groves among.

### 19

Ye perish'd joys, why like the meteor fair
Did ye once blaze, but only blaze to die?
Like exhalations in the summer's sky
Ye have dissolv'd in air.

### 20

Where are ye fled, ye fascinating hours?
Disport ye gaily on the northern breeze
Wave ye your fragrant wings where chrystal Tees
Salutes her winding shores.

### 21

Or with adventurous flight do ye explore
The clime where Avon's silent waters flow
Where ancient Bladud's tepid fountains glow
With vivifying power?

### 22

But are ye fled for ever, shall dispair
With canker'd tooth corrode this heart forlorn?
The crimson dawn of hope, predicts a morn
In fancy's visions fair.

### 23

Tho' dark the prospect hope will intervene;
As when at times auspicious sunbeams smile
Thro' sullen mists and feebly gild awhile
The distant watery scene.

### 24

O balmy hours ye will once more arrive;
The flower of joy that bends before the gust
And weeps her blossoms scatter'd in the dust
Shall with your breath revive.

[pp.296-98]. *c*.1807, but possibly later (?1810-1815). "The Minstrel's Lament" appears to be addressed to Elizabeth Russell, whose residence at Hardwicke, near the 'crystal Tees', is alluded to in stanza 20; Elizabeth took the waters at Bath ('Bladud', stanza 21).

George included an eleven stanza version of "The Minstrel's Lament" with the copy of his "Verses Addressed to a Lady on Her Departure" sent to his niece Julia in the mid to late 1820s (L.A.O. T.d'E.H 152/2). Stanza 21, which refers to Elizabeth Russell, is omitted. Two new concluding stanzas (10 and 11) are added:

Ah how should I pursue th'enlivening strain
And weave the forms of hope in fancy's loom?
How gild with orient light the midnight gloom
Alas! th'attempt is vain.

For she is fled for aye, who bade me sweep
The breathing chords of my devoted lyre
And irresponsive to its master's fire
The harp but wakes to weep.

The following additional changes have been made to the stanzas: 15 (1) line 1 'their' replaced by 'thy'; 16 (2) line 3 'sorrow's' replaced by 'pity's'; 24 (9) line 1 'arrive' replaced by 'revive', line 2 'that' replaced by 'which' and line 3 'in' replaced by 'to'. George adds a footnote to stanza 17 (3) line 1 ('Sweet as the perfume of the fading rose') 'N.b. The rose is sweetest when fading.' Punctuation is altered slightly.

### *The Wandering Jew* [Fig. 7]

1

O stranger, why inquire the hapless fate
Of one most surely scath'd by power supreme
My guilt past utterance why should I relate
Or tale of woe will bid these eyes to stream
With pity's kindly drops[?] - my fortunes teem
With incidents so horrible and rare
That thou incredulous perchance may'st deem
Reason divested of her throne and care
And age to have installed second childhood there.

2

And yet this stedfast eye no sign betrays
Of intellectual frenzy or decay
My memory is firm and tells of days
In dark oblivion long pass'd away;
When Rome submitted to Augustus' sway
I first drew breath and oh! that in my spring
The bud of life had withered for aye[!]
Oh! that e'en now at last oh heavenly king
Thou would'st in mercy deign to snap this vital string[!]

3

Ah! not thro' ignorance I sinn'd but pride;
I bow before thy righteous judgments, Lord!
I saw thy works and yet thy power denied
Contemn'd thy threat'nings and despis'd thy word;
Thy lowly guise my carnal heart abhorr'd;
O yet at last revoke thy fearful doom
Let mercy temper judgment, let thy sword
Of vengeance slumber, and the silent tomb
My ever tortur'd heart and wearied limbs enwomb.[4]

---

[4]  Subsequently altered to 'This ever sleepless eye and withered heart enwomb.'

4

How vain the prayer! I bear a charmed life,
I tarry till he comes; such the decree
Of him who sav'd the world, and neither knife
Rope[,] rack, nor pois'nous herb, nor malady
Fire, earth[,] nor air can ever set me free;
When blood and water issued from his side
'Twas I who pierc'd him on the fatal tree
And therefore now a wretched deicide
Deathless and vagabond I wander far and wide.

5

And on my brow[,] an ever burning spear
Fed by the self renew'd and anguish'd brain
Adown these furrow'd cheeks the scalding tear
Compels, and bids me woefully complain;
Ah! who can live in never ending pain?
Yet till the great Archangel's trump shall call
The dead to judgment, must I still sustain
This fiery torment; till this earthly ball
Enwrapt by flames shall shrivel like a parched scroll.

6

Ye mortals, insects of life's little day
Of brief and puny sorrows why complain[?]
Awhile ye flutter in the solar ray
And die at eve - soon is your mingled skein
Unwound, and fate divides the thread in twain;
Ye deem your joys and woes shall ever last,
Your hopes are fruitless, as your fears are vain
Ye burst like bubbles on the ocean vast
Of dread eternity - the dream of life is past.

*or*

Ye mortals, insects of life's little day
Your brief and puny sorrows why deplore?
Awhile ye wanton in the sultry ray
Or mourn with drooping wing the passing show'r
And die what time bright Hesper doth restore
The evening grey - soon is your mingled skein
Unwound by destiny, resistless power[,]
And pitying death divides the thread in twain;
But I in this dark world for ever must remain.

[pp.300-01]. ?1815-25. George's version omits line 5 of the alternative final stanza - this has been reinstated using the draft on page 637. The drafts have also been quarried to help restore George's punctuation (shown in square brackets). Printed without the alternative final stanza in 'Tennyson's father', pp. 292-94, and in full (though omitting the missing line, discussed above) by Tennyson & Dyson, pp.47-49. George's Commonplace Book contains numerous versions of the stanzas: pp.608-09 (1-5), 616-17 (1 and 2), 647 (6), 661 (6), 665 (6, Fig. 8). A version of "The Wandering Jew" is included in Thomas Percy's *Reliques of Ancient Poetry* (London, 1765); the 1823 edition (?replacing an earlier copy) is in George's library at T.R.C. George also owned John Brand's *Observations on Popular Antiquities* (1810 edn, London) which discusses the legend. George K. Anderson, *The Legend of the Wandering Jew* (Providence, 1965) and Edgar Rosenberg, *From Shylock to Svengali: Jewish Stereotypes in English Fiction* (Stanford, 1960) demonstrate how the story of Ahasuerus, the Wandering Jew, featured prominently in literature of the period: in 'Monk' Lewis' *The Monk* (London, 1796); in Southey's *The Curse of Kehama* (London, 1810); in Shelley's *St. Irvyne, or the Rosicrucian* (London, 1811), *Queen Mab* (London, 1813), *Alastor* (London, 1816), and *Hellas* (London, 1822); in the 'Rev. T. Clark' [i.e. John Galt], *The Wandering Jew* (London, 1820); and in Byron's *Cain* (London, 1821). The difficulty remains in identifying George's direct influences, and hence the date of the poem.

The following stanzas (p.619) might be part of "The Wandering Jew" (see also the discussion of "It is the lot of man").

> O'er frozen seas thro' torrid regions borne
> Alternate, either by the bitter blast
> Transpierc'd or smitten by the flame, forlorn
> That century of varying woe I pass'd;
> Woe worse from sudden contrast, while with haste
> Swift as aetherial flash, my restless flight
> The fiend impelled, from where for ever fast
> In chrystal chains pale Saturn lies and night
> Eternal reigns, to where mercurial ardors smite.
>
> And thence to Saturn's utmost verge, our path
> Aerial we retrace; a wretched prey
> To that fell demon, all the varied wrath
> Of fierce extremes I knew, and no allay
> Assuaged the wintry blast or fiery ray;
> And still had I been subject to his power
> But as we pass'd heav'n's gates, th'angelic lay
> Stole on the ravish'd sense and then no more
> The fiend his victim grasp'd but fled in happy hour.

---

Figure 7 (pp.78-79): "The Wandering Jew". George Clayton Tennyson's Commonplace Book, pp. 300-01 (Tennyson Research Centre Collection).

Figure 8 (pp.80-81): Drafts for "It is the lot of man" and "The Wandering Jew" with drawings - the ground plan is possibly the Rectory at Somerby. George Clayton Tennysons's Commonplace Book, pp. 664-65 (Tennyson Research Centre Collection).

300

The wandering Jew

1

O Stranger, why enquire the hapless fate
of one most sorely beaten by power supreme
My guilt past utterance why should I relate
or tale of woe will bid thine eyes to stream      eyelids
With pity's kindly drops – my fortunes teem
With incidents so horrible and rare
That thou incredulous perchance may'st deem
Reason divested of her throne and care,
And Age to have installed second childhood there

2

And yet this stedfast eye no sign betrays
Of intellectual frenzy or decay
My memory is firm and tells of days
In dark oblivion long pass'd away;
When Rome submitted to Augustus' sway
I first drew breath and oh! that in my spring
The bud of life had withered for age
Oh! that e'en now at last oh heavenly king
Thou would'st in mercy so deign to snap this vital string.

3

ah! not this ignorance I sinn'd but pride;
I bow before thy righteous judgments, Lord!
I saw thy works and yet thy power denied
Contemn'd thy threat'nings & despised thy word:
Thy lowly guise my carnal heart abhorr'd:
O yet at last revoke thy fearful doom
Let mercy temper judgment, let thy sword
Of vengeance slumber, & the silent tomb
<del>My over beating heart</del> & <del>wearied limbs</del> enwomb.
This    sleepless eyes      withered heart

4

How vain the prayer! I bear a charmed life,
I tarry till he comes; such the decree
Of him who said the world, and neither knife
Nope rack, nor poisonous herb. nor malady
Fire, earth nor air can ever set me free;
When blood & water issued from his side
'Twas I who pierc'd him on the fatal tree
And therefore now a wretched heicide
Deathless and vagabond I wander far & wide

78

5

301

And on my brow an ever burning spear
Fed by the self renew'd and anguish'd brain
Adown these furrow'd cheeks the scalding tear
Compels, and bids me woefully complain;
Ah! who can live in never ending pain?
Yet till the great Archangel's trump shall call
The dead to judgment, must I still sustain
This fiery torment; till this earthly ball
Enwrapt by flames shall shrivel like a scorched scroll.

6

Ye mortals, insects of life's little day
Of brief & puny sorrows why complain
Awhile ye flutter in in the solar ray,
And die at eve — soon is your mingled skein
Unwound, & fate divides the thread in twain;
Ye deem your joys & woes shall ever last,
Your hopes are fruitless, as your fears are vain,
Ye burst like bubbles on the ocean vast
Of dread Eternity — the dream of life is past.

or

Ye mortals, insects of life's little day
Your brief & puny sorrows why deplore?
Awhile ye wanton in the sultry ray
And die when their bright Hesper doth restore
The evening grey — soon is your mingled skein
Unwound by destiny resistless power
And palsyno Death divides the thread in twain
But See this dark world for ever must uneasy.

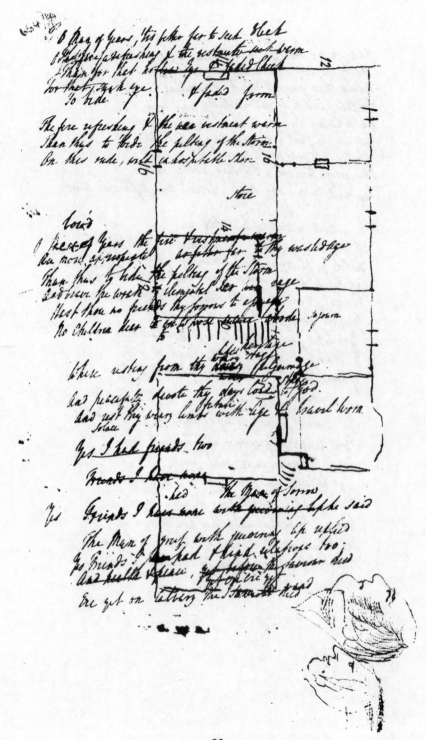

665

Ye mortels insects of lifes little day
of brief & puny sorrows why complain?
Awhile ye flutter in the solar ray
And die at eve; soon is your mingled skein
Of life unwound & fate divides the thread in twain
Ye deem your joys & woes shall ever last.
Your hopes are fruitless as your fears are vain
Ye burst like bubbles in the breeze vast
Of dead Eternity — & the dream of life is past.

O for that hollow Eye & wasted form     solacing
More fit the vestments warm, & free unwasting
than thus to bide the peltry of the storm
                        of its rude embracing
Hast thou no friends to whom thy steps retiring
                with                      calesfacing
Thy wearied limbs may rest with ser trifin warm
                                        embracing

No children dear, with head come    refacing
                                        defacing
                                        displacing
                                        ifacing
                                        o'facing

O ye mortels

Ye mortels
         the insects of life's little day
of brief & puny sorrows why complain?
Awhile ye flutter in the solar ray     party coloured
                        how soon
And dye at eventide quickly your skein
Is looped & yet strange thoughts ye calculate frign sugn
                                                    vein
as tho' your joys & woes should ever last.
Your hopes how fruitless & your fears how vain.
Ye float like bubbles on the breeze vast
And burst — The dream of life is over & all is past.

                    how soon mingled
And dye at eve — your party coloured skein
Is wound

And dye at eve — soon is your mingled skein
Of good & ill) by fate unwound
unwound

81

*Il Penseroso*

I

O Muse of rapture! that delightful strain
Those tones that with the Teian chords conspire
To make such dulcet music breathe again,
Again with sportive fingers sweep the lyre
Thy voice attuning to the trembling wire
O sing of odours, sing of joy and love
Of thousand sweets that spring from soft desire
Of graceful nymphs that in the myrtle grove
With rosy chaplets crown'd in airy measures move.

II

As when the winds of heaven disperse the shower
The lowering landscape brightens to the day
The sun suffus'd in tears awhile, once more
Looks out serene and sheds his brilliant ray
O'er lucid streams and fields and forests gay
Thus oft, full oft thy magic minstrelsy
Enchantress blest! has charm'd my cares away
Bid from my brow the chords of sorrow fly
And laughter loving pleasure sparkle in mine eye.

[p.304]. ?c.1811-20.

*The Battle of the Hydaspes*

List, India, list! was that the trumpet's breath
That rang so dreadful on the loaded gale?
Whence the bright gleam that flashes on mine eye
Where old Hydaspes pours his golden wave?
He comes! young Ammon, on whose laurelled brow
Ambition sits enthron'd; ambition nerv'd
His red right arm, when late on Issus' plain
He crush'd the monarch of the eastern world.
Darius!
He, girt with pomp and useless pageantry

[p.309]. Unfinished. ?c.1810-20. The Hydaspes, a river in the Punjab, was the scene of Alexander the Great's last major pitched battle in 326 B.C.; Alexander had defeated Darius at Issus in 333 B.C. Apart from Xenophon, George also owned Charles Rollin's *Ancient History*, 8 vols (1789). Cf. Alfred Tennyson's "Persia", "The High-Priest to Alexander" (both printed in *Poems by Two Brothers* of 1827) and "Alexander" (c.1832).

# POEMS BY GEORGE CLAYTON TENNYSON

[*It is the lot of man*]

### 1

It is the lot[5] of man by sin defac'd
To taste of various sorrows from the womb
Yet oft blue violets paint this earthly waste
And in this wilderness gay roses bloom
Scenting the desart air with rich perfume;
It is a mingled destiny we share
E'en from the puling cradle to the tomb
Such our vicissitude of dark and fair
Our lot is cast upon the chequer'd chessboard's square.

### 2

There are to whom in mercy or in ire
High heaven hath bid woe's chalice overflow
Who drink in copious draughts the ferment dire
And drain th'envenom'd dregs - these undergo
All the variety of ills below
That spring from poverty, contempt and pain
Remorse with scorpions bound about her brow
And jealousy with murder in his train
And baleful envy pining at another's gain.[6]

### 3

There are who barely skim the cup of sorrow
And gay thro' life's enamell'd path advance
Whose jocund hearts forgetful of tomorrow
The festive bowl, the song, the wreathed dance
And lovely woman's witching smiles entrance;
Ah! do they dream their joys shall ever last?
Tho' sunbeams smile thro' ether's blue expanse
Too soon is their horizon overcast
And all their blossoms scatter'd to the whirlwind's blast.

### 4

The shining snake conceals the poison fell
The rosebud hides the worm, a thorn the rose;
Say would'st thou know where festering corses dwell?
With mimic life where Parian marble glows
And gilded laurels deck the warrior's brows.

5  Subsequently altered to 'fate'.
6  George indicates that the final line should be replaced with 'And madness harassing the mind with fancies vain'.

Then when the bowl is mantling to the brim
And sparkling wine from chrystal goblets flows
Demoniac frenzy dances on the rim
Despair and ruin on the smiling surface swim.

[p.642]. The possibly strong autobiographical element suggests a date of c.1815-25. A fifth stanza is numbered but not transcribed by G. C. Tennyson. Like "The Wandering Jew" this material was much reworked. The original germ appears to be a version of the first three stanzas which begins: 'Each child of man is born of woe to taste / Train'd up in various sorrows from the womb' (p.662). A slightly modified version ('It is the lot of man by sin defac'd / To taste of various sorrows from the womb'), itself heavily revised (p.656), is followed by a number of additional numbered stanzas (pp.656-57 and 659):

As late I wandered near the vexed shore
To view the wild winds with the waves contending
To hear the seamews with the ocean's roar,
Their harsh and melancholy accents blending
I saw an aged form in sorrow bending
Thro' his hoar tresses moan'd the hollow gale
And the last watery solar ray descending
Gleam'd on a countenance so sad and pale
Methought some tenant of the tomb had burst his vail.

Whilome I journey'd much through various lands
From western Gades to remote Cathay
From where parch'd Nubia spreads her burning sands
And nations bask in India's sultry ray
To Zembla's snows and Tornio's frozen bay
Yet did I never see a cheek so wan
In all my wanderings near and far away
It was a mere anatomy of man
With awe yet pity I address'd and thus began

"O for that hollow eye, and wasted form
More fit the vestment warm, and potion cheering,
Than thus to bide the pelting of the storm
The bitter sleet from angry clouds careering
Is there no one with sympathy endearing
Will intermingle friendly tears with thine
No child or kin, with kindness persevering
Will smooth thy pillow now thy days decline
Art thou of all bereft, survivor of thy line?

Much have I suffered in this world of tears,
And learnt by woe for other's woe to feel,
Immur'd for twenty hopeless tedious years,
In mouldy dungeons of the dark Bastille,
Where the red drops that warm the heart congeal;

At Goa by Rome's hellhounds apprehended,
Demons with hands of blood and hearts of steel,
And thrice upon the rack of pain contended,
Till the wrench'd sinews burst, and life awhile was ended[").

George subsequently cancelled the final line of the penultimate stanza in this group 'Art thou
of all bereft, survivor of thy line?' replacing it with 'And to thy wearied limbs a home of rest
assign.' The cancelled line became the germ of the last, unfinished, stanza in this sequence ('Or
art thou reft of all, by all deserted / The crumbling structure of a former day'), itself developed
further on p.646:

He seem'd of all bereft, by all deserted
In this world's wilderness a pilgrim lone;
His wildered look betrayed a mind subverted
And that of reason's arch the good keystone
Had been by misery and age o'erthrown.
Yet the bright flashes from his eyes that broke
Said, here the gems of wit and wisdom shone
Till shiver'd quite by frenzy's vengeful stroke
Yet ev'n the fragments bright their former worth bespoke.

He seem'd of all bereft, by all forsaken
Like some lorn structure of a former day
From whose disjointed stones and turrets shaken
The lated trav'll'r turns in haste away
Contemplating far its turrets gray.
It was not thus in wassal days of yore
Now thro' the halls where swell'd the minstrel's lay
Or sunk in melting cadence, tempests roar
And shrieks the boding owl where ladies sang before.

Now the fang'd adder winds his fearful road
Thro' the rank weeds which clasp the mouldring hall
Where titled dames and crested barons trod
The mazy dance in hours of festival
And thro' the grass-grown courts gaunt wolves appal
With ravening glare, where once from beauty's eye
Stole the soft glance that did the heart enthrall.
There's nought beneath heavn's ample canopy
But falls by time to wreck, how strong so e'er it be.

As G. C. Tennyson reworked the material for "It is the lot of man", all these additional stanzas
were abandoned and a fourth stanza 'The shining snake conceals the poison fell' developed. "It
is the lot of man" is followed (p.644) by further draft stanzas:

Near that bituminous lake in Palestine
Yclept Asphaltites, as legends tell
Fair apples grow, with plump and blushing skin

85

On this wide earth without a parallel
Smooth to the touch and pleasant to the smell;
Yet they are nought within but ashes vile
Tho' to the view they others far excell;
And such is woman with her glavering smile
For all is fair without but all within is guile.

Yet one I knew, but she is gone for aye
From these fond arms by fate untimely torn
Pure as the snow 'ere kiss'd by Phoebus' ray
Or gemmy dewdrop spangling to the morn;
Guileless as cherub infant newly born;
Enrich'd by all that culture could impart
To form the manners and the mind adorn;
By nature blest beyond the rules of art
With woman's brightest ornament a guileless heart.

A final, unfinished, stanza ('Yet did the beauty of her person vie / Those houri nymphs whom Mussulmen extol / While thro' the heaven of her dark blue eye / Shone her transcendant loveliness of soul') is probably related to the following (p.701; drafts pp.701-02)

Yet she was fair all other nymphs excelling
Matchless in grace, supreme in loveliness,
In form as exquisite, as houris dwelling
Pavilion'd in the radiant pearls recess
Whom doting Moslems deem they shall possess
In blissful climes beneath the throne of God.
Yes even female envy may confess
Now she lies low, commingling with the clod
That she was peerless all and beautiful as good.

Many of these additional stanzas have very much the feel of being part of what may tentatively be called "The Wandering Jew" sequence. Indeed some drafts of the final stanza of "The Wandering Jew" are to be found in these pages of George's Commonplace Book.

[*What Anthony's imperial pomp o'erthrew*]

What Anthony's imperial pomp o'erthrew
What him whose giant strength at Ascalon
A thousand of his country's foemen slew
His worthless weapon but an asses bone?
For all the glories which his arm had won
By gentile lords with daily travail worn
And doom'd in Gaza's dungeon damps to groan
Once proud Philistia's dread and then her scorn
That Nazarite of yore of strength and eye sight shorn.

[p.649] Written on a page ruled for a list (?of communicants) dated December 1818. A version of the story of Samson (*Judges*, 13-16). This Spenserian stanza (with variants on p.648) might also be related to "The Wandering Jew" sequence.

*Song*

I am mad Tom, I know it
And sometimes I am furious
But I am wise and rule the skies
Orion, Sol, Arcturus.

What tho' folks point I'm wiser
Than e'er was mortal found
I rule the moon in her high noon
And whirl the planets round.

I'll climb those lofty mountains
And there I'll fight the gypsies
I'll play at bowls with the sun and moon
And kick them to eclipses.

I'll climb yon lofty mountains
In spite of wind and weather
I'll tear the rainbow from the skies
And splice both ends together.

What tho' I'm poor I'll marry
And then poor Tom will sing
For Saturn rolls by my command
And I'll marry with his ring.

I have no dirty acres
To settle on my love
But the flaming fields of space are mine
And the canopy above.

With heaven's studded concave
I'll bind her forehead fair
Her eyes shall be the northern lights
And a comet's tail her hair.

Oh then I'll breed a riot
And be a merry loon
With mountains I'll at ninepins play
And trundle with the moon.

[pp.688-89]. ?c.1815-25. Printed: 'Alfred's father', pp.294-95 and Tennyson & Dyson, pp.53-55, where it is (erroneously) suggested 'eclipses' (stanza 3, line 4) should perhaps be 'ellipses'. In the manuscript, stanzas 3 and 4 are bracketed together. George cancelled the start of a further stanza:

> The rainbow for a garter
> I'll bind around her knee

Six mad songs, including "Old Tom of Bedlam" were printed in Thomas Percy's *Reliques of Ancient Poetry*; the edition of 1823 is at T.R.C. See also Frank Sidgwick, 'Tom of Bedlam's Song', *London Mercury* (7 March 1923), pp.518-24. George was probably also using a popular song. Byron's *Letters to **** ****** on the Rev. W.L. Bowles' Strictures on the Life and Writings of Pope* (London, 1821) has as an epigraph:

> "I'll play at *Bowls* with the Sun and Moon"
>
> OLD SONG

Andrew Nicholson (ed.), *Lord Byron. The Complete Miscellaneous Prose* (Oxford, 1991), p.411, has traced a four-stanza version of this song, 'I'll sail upon the Dog-star', in *The Vocal Miscellany...*, 3rd edn (Dublin, 1738), pp.229-30:

> I'll sail upon the Dog-star,
>     And then pursue the Morning;
> I'll chase the Moon 'till it be Noon,
>     I'll make her leave her horning.
>
> I'll climb the frosty Mountain,
>     And there I'll coin the Weather:
> I'll tear the Rain-bow from the Sky,
>     And tie both Ends together.
>
> The Stars pluck from their Orbs too,
>     And crowd them in my Budget;
> And whether I'm a roaring Boy,
>     Let *Gresham*-College judge it.
>
> While I mount yon blue Coelum,
>     To shun the tempting Gipsies;
> Play at Foot-ball with Sun and Moon,
>     And fright ye with Eclipses.

A version of George's "Mad Tom" stanzas exists in the manuscript of Alfred's "The Coach of Death" of the mid 1820s. This is printed in facsimile in Christopher Ricks and Aidan Day (eds.), *Tennyson. The Manuscripts at the Beinecke Library Yale University*, Tennyson Archive, XXIV (New York, 1990), pp.14-15, where it is suggested the hand is not Alfred's. To the present writers it appears to be very much in Alfred's youthful handwriting. George's second and last stanzas are omitted; 'yon' is replaced by 'those' (stanza 4, line 1). Stanza 5 reads:

What tho' I'm poor I'll marry
And then glad Tom shall sing
For Saturn rolls at my command
I'll marry with his ring

This is followed by a new stanza:

I have no gold nor jewels
Nor money at command
I'll deck me in the sun's bright beams
Who'll then refuse my hand

# II. OTHER MANUSCRIPT POETRY

*A Perfectly New Chorus[,] Strophe and Antistrophe -wise[,]
from the Clerk and Advocate to Their Beloved Sister in the North*

Strophe 1
1 While you serene
2 Do sit and muse
3 Mid sylvan shade
4 'Neath some tall oak
5 Or spiry larch
6 Tranquil and calm
7 Apart

Antistrophe 1
1 We lank and lean
2 Do rather chuse
3 Intent to wade
4 Thro' Blackstone, Coke,
5 Or comments starch
6 Of bible, balm
7 Of heart

Strophe 2
1 While you the mind
2 Do cultivate
3 From authors sage
4 Do wisely cull
5 Like honey'd bee
6 The choicest sweets
7 Of petal

Antistrophe 2
1 With poring blind
2 Early and late
3 Like Persian mage
4 We fill the skull
5 Of H— and B—
6 Avoiding treats
7 And meat all

Strophe 3
1 Costly to dine,
2 A second course
3 Of some is theme -
4 Meanwhile they swill
5 Wine till top full -
6 They hogsheads pour
7 Down greedy throat -

Antistrophe 3
1 Thus some opine
2 Good eating source
3 Of joy supreme -
4 While book worms fill
5 Their paper skull
6 With crabbed lore
7 Not worth a groat -

Strophe 4 - Sublimely unintelligible
1 O Phoebus bright
2 Whose partial day
3 Effulgent shines
4 O'er wisdom's fane
5 [Or o'er the bower
6 Where Spartan moise
7 Is vis a vis

Antistrophe 4
1 To that fam'd light
2 Achain's ray
3 Whom golden mines
4 Could not restrain
5 From risking power
6 Of Lydian croise,
7 And his avis

Strophe 5
1 Did nobly give;
2 Or o'er the stream
3 Where Uncle Nep -
4 With eye balls meek,
5 The king of whale
6 O'er trout and ling
7 Doth gaze]

Antistrophe 5
1 O while I live
2 Benignly beam
3 My devious step
4 To guide - I seek
5 That happy vale
6 Where Muses sing
7 Their lays.

Strophe 6
1 Where gladsome song
2 The muses nine
3 Melodious pour
4 From golden strings
5 Where Helicon
6 Meand'ring strays
7 In many a rill.

Antistrophe 6
1 These nymphs among
2 O be it mine
3 To sit each hour
4 While musick rings -
5 And every one
6 On fiddle plays
7 On Parnass-hill.

L.A.O. T.d'E. H 152/3. In G. C. Tennyson's hand (and may be largely his composition). Dates from after November 1806 when Charles was called to the Bar (manuscript is not watermarked). Another work addressed to Elizabeth Russell. Blackstone and Coke (Antistrophe 1) were legal treatises. The square brackets are George's.

[*Unsullied Album*]

Unsullied album, may no thought unholy
Thy fair untainted purity distain,
May no unhallow'd hand with touch of folly
Thy pages, emblem of her mind, profane.
When candour, truth and innocence combin'd
In pleasing amity a dwelling find.

But here may fancy all her charms unfold,
And lull the mourner with her vision bright
Fringe sorrow's sable stole with inwrought gold
And tip dejection's dusky wings with light.
Till hope emerge from pale affliction's gloom
And flowers of joy bedeck the darkness of the tomb.

L.A.O. T.d'E. H 152/2. A manuscript sent to 'Miss Julia Tennyson' with untitled copies of the "Verses Addressed to a Lady on Her Departure" and "The Minstrel's Lament" ('Sweet is thy memory'). These copies of George's (favourite) verses originally addressed to Elizabeth Russell date from the mid to late 1820s. "Unsullied Album" was added by Julia's father to the manuscript. It is unlikely to be his work and would appear to be George's composition. Cf. stanza 2, line 6, with cancelled versions of 'Sweet is thy memory', stanza 10 (above, p.74), line 3: 'How cheer the eternal darkness/silence of the tomb', 'How gild with sober rays the midnight gloom' and 'How gild the mouldring fragments of the tomb'. The Somersby Tennysons certainly sent birthday verses to Julia. In January 1831 she wrote to her grandfather: 'According to my promise, my dear Grand Papa, I send you a copy of the verses which Alfred wrote on my birth-day, although you predicted I should forget it as soon as I left Tealby...' (L.A.O. 2T.d'E. H87/9 - the verses no longer survive). "Unsullied Album", which the authors believe unlikely to be Alfred's lost poem (a possible candidate is "To — [Sainted Juliet!]", published in 1830), might date from the mid to late 1820s, but could equally well be a copy of some earlier stanzas of George's (and addressed to Elizabeth Russell?).

# EUSTACE; AN ELEGY (1851)
## by
## Charles Tennyson d'Eyncourt

Published and printed for Tennyson d'Eyncourt, whose name does not appear on the title-page, by William Davy and Son, 8 Gilbert Street, Oxford Street (some first editions are dated 1850). The second edition, also of 1851, was published by Saunders and Otley, Conduit Street - Davy remained the printer. The title-page has an epigraph from Horace: 'Quis desiderio sit pudor aut modus / tam cari capitis?' [*Odes*, I, XXIV: 'What shame or limit could there be to the grief for a life so dear?'].

The volume contains four plates by the lithographers Dickinson and Co. (Figs. 6, 10, 11, 12) and one engraving in the text. William Davy and Son issued a second edition in the same year.

All Tennyson d'Eyncourt's footnotes have been reproduced in this edition.

[p.iii]

DEDICATED
TO MY BELOVED SISTER
### ELIZABETH RUSSELL,
IN GRATEFUL REMEMBRANCE OF
HER WARM AFFECTION FOR
MY LAMENTED SON,
AND OF THE CONSOLATION I DERIVED
FROM HER GENTLE SYMPATHY
IN THE HOUR OF GRIEF.

C.d'E.

[p.v] THIS ELEGY is an expanded translation of the following lines inscribed on a deep-sounding Clock-Bell, cast in 1842, immediately after the death at Barbadoes, — of CAPTAIN EUSTACE d'EYNCOURT, aged 25, who fell victim to Yellow Fever within a few days after he had arrived from England to join his Regiment.
The Clock and Bell are placed in one of the Towers of Bayons Manor, Lincolnshire, the residence of his family. —

ME POSUIT
CAROLUS DE EYNCOURT,
FILIUM, FLORE ÆTATIS ABREPTUM,
### EUSTACHIUM DILECTISSIMUM
DEFLENS.
REVOCET VOX MEA DULCES AMORIS HORAS: —
MONEAT QUOQUE — QUAM FUGACES!
QUANTULA SIT VITA!

[I was set here by Charles d'Eyncourt, in mourning for his most beloved son, Eustace, taken from him in the flower of his youth. May my sound recall the sweet hours of love; but warn too how fleeting they are. How short is life!]

———

As in the Original, the BELL is supposed to speak, throughout the Poem.

———

POEMS BY TWO BROTHERS

## EPITAPH

ON A MONUMENT ERECTED IN THE CHANCEL OF THE PARISH
CHURCH OF TEALBY, IN THE COUNTY OF LINCOLN.

To the Memory of

### EUSTACE ALEXANDER TENNYSON D'EYNCOURT,

CAPTAIN IN THE 46TH REGIMENT,
WHO DIED AT BARBADOES,
ON THE 9TH MARCH
1842,
AGED 25 YEARS.

HE WAS
THE FOURTH AND YOUNGEST SURVIVING SON OF
THE RIGHT HONORABLE

### CHARLES TENNYSON D'EYNCOURT,
AND FRANCES MARY HIS WIFE.

HIS GENEROUS SPIRIT, VIGOROUS INTELLECT
AND NOBLE QUALITIES,
PROMISED TO ADORN THE HIGH CAREER
TO WHICH THE ENERGY AND FIRMNESS
OF HIS CHARACTER
SEEMED TO DESTINE HIM ;
WHILE HIS MANLY BEARING,
GENTLE NATURE AND WINNING GRACE,
ENDEARED HIM TO HIS COMRADES
AND TO ALL WITH WHOM HE LIVED.

TENDERLY BELOVED
BY HIS PARENTS AND FAMILY,
THIS MONUMENT RECORDS THEIR GRIEF,
AND ILLUSTRATES THE INSTABILITY
OF EARTHLY BLESSINGS.

HIS REMAINS ARE DEPOSITED IN THE CEMETERY
OF ST. PAUL'S CHURCH, BARBADOES.

Figure 9: Memorial to Eustace Tennyson d'Eyncourt (1816-1842) from Charles
Tennyson d'Eyncourt's *Eustace (1851)* [p. vi].

Figure 10: Tower at Bayons Manor, in which was placed the Clock-bell
commemorating Eustace Tennyson d'Eyncourt. Lithograph by Dickinson and Co.
for Charles Tennyson d'Eyncourt's *Eustace (1851)*.

## CANTO I

———

*"Filium, flore ætatis abreptum,*
*EUSTACHIUM dilectissimum*
*deflens."*

———

How calm is Life, while yet in soft repose, —
Forgetful of its Fate, untaught by woes,
Nor wakened by the Voice of Time, — it sweetly flows!

When pain and sorrow come, they stir the mind
To think of Destiny: — but Man is blind,
During the Sunshine of his brief career,
Save to the flowers which at his feet appear.
Swiftly, the blast each fragrant bloom bereaves,
Where smiled the blossoms, — lie the withered leaves!

Wherefore, a Father who hath deeply mourned
A Gallant Son, with every Grace adorned,
Swept from the Earth in Manhood's flow'ry prime, —
Now warns his race to heed the march of Time:
To mark — that every step curtails the span,
By Nature's Law assigned to Mortal Man;
That when my Voice proclaims in Solemn tone
The passing Hour, — *an Hour of Life is gone!*

Alas! each stroke of Time but sounds the Knell
Of Scenes for ever past! — and who can tell
What awful change the Hour now creeping on
May bring! In it, — the ills you may have done
Repair! — In some such petty space, before
My Tongue shall hence declare another Hour,
Time with his measured step — unfailing — true, —
Inexorable Time — will claim his due:
And when that Hour — to all who live around,
Shall be pronounced complete, — the pealing sound
Whose sweet vibrations, for revolving years,
Had roused your energies or soothed your cares,
Will fail to reach you on that distant shore,
Where, — as a Thing of Time, — you live no more!

But yet the Things of Time — though born to die, —
He seeks to perfect, ere he would destroy;
If Man's whole Race — and Worlds shall pass away, —

# EUSTACE; AN ELEGY

Each has a purpose ere it must obey
The General Law which dooms it to decay.
Time o'er them claims a transitory reign: —
Rejoices in his Subjects when they gain
A full maturity for Nature's End, —
And mourns when Fate shall interfere to rend
A Tissue woven by his mystic power,
Even to form the cradle for a Flower,
Whose fragrant bosom might a Charm distil,
Its brief — but heavenly Mission to fulfil,
By gladdening unseen myriads in the air,
Ere Sunset close their whole existence here!

How must he grieve when nobler works shall fail!
And now — he bids me, in his name, bewail
The wreck of One he fashioned to adorn
His fleeting Realm! — Full oft, in Spring, — the Morn
With gentle breath and sunny smile conveys
A hope, its lurking storm ere Noon betrays.

I call the echoes from the silent Hills:
My searching note each peaceful Valley fills:
Those Hills where Eustace, yet a Child, would play; —
The Vallies, where, a Youth, he loved to stray.
O'er the broad Woods the cadence rolls along: —
The Wild Birds hear it and suspend their Song;
For in those Woods and Groves on Wold and Plain,
He dreamt of Life and Love, — and dreamt in vain!
There would he muse on Glory — and on Fame:
There, — as a Soldier, fancy that his name
Might grace his Country's annals, — and impart
Some proud emotion to a Parent's heart.
Commingled with such dreamings, — Whispers oft,
Of Joy, — would reach his Soul; — and Visions soft —
Pure as his Nature, or an Angel's breath:
A shadow veiled them! — 'twas Thy Shadow, Death!
The Fame and Glory were, alas! denied:—
How to deserve them, he had learnt, — and died!
But those the Whispers and the Visions rare
Which to the Few their destiny declare:
The dim presentiments of second birth
To joys ineffable, — beyond the Earth!
Thus may a glimpse of future bliss be given
To some, — the Pure and Good — th' Elect of Heaven!

Figure 11: Eustace's funeral in Barbados, 1842. Lithograph by Dickinson and Co. for Charles Tennyson d'Eyncourt's *Eustace (1851)*.

# EUSTACE; AN ELEGY

Eustace! for Thee, — such bliss may be in store: —
And those who now thy Earthly fate deplore,
May, if they live to toil through age and care, —
Dream of thee — then — as of a Vision fair—
Which glided from this darkening scene away,
Ere Sin or Sorrow dulled the bright array,
Wherein thy graceful form embalmed remains
In Memory's Shrine: — for even Time retains
No Power to blight it there!
                                            If so they dream, —
Then may they cease to weep for thee, — and deem
Most happy, those, who live to taste the joy
Of youthful hope — and ere it withers — die!

In a far Isle was drawn thy latest breath:
No anxious Brother watched thy bed of Death;
Though Comrades all thy feverish wants supplied,
The Loved and Loving stood not by thy side.
Thy failing hand, no gentle Sister pressed,
Thy head reposed not on a Mother's breast;
Thy dying accents found no Father's ear,
No weeping Household gathered round thy bier.
Yet, — when the death-drum rolled a deep farewell, —
And the swift volley boomed the Soldier's knell, —
Though not one Kindred tear bedewed thy Grave,
Thy Spirit claimed a kindred with the Brave!
Heaved many a breast which war in vain had steeled;
Around thee drooped the Stoics of the Field, —
And Veterans taught all forms of death to see
With eyes unmoistened, — wept aloud for thee!
For while, in Duty — to thyself severe,
Thy gracious nature could Command endear;
And, when thy voice was silenced in the dust,
Their Love recalled the Merciful and Just.
Love for the Just — the wildest bosoms learn: —
Mercy will find its Mourners in the Stern.

Nor lonely lyest thou in that distant Grave,
For Heaven, in Death, a dear Companion gave;
One who had shared thy pleasures and thy pains,
True to thee Living — True in Death remains.
On that same fatal night — thy Mordaunt dies:
So linked your fates — that he beside thee lies; —

99

In Peace, together sleep — in Joy, together rise! [1]

## CANTO II

———

*"Revocat Vox mea dulces amoris horas."*

———

Ah! what is Life! — scarce forty days before,
His presence graced the scene in Bayons Tower.
Four hundred joyful guests a banquet shared,
In all the form of olden times prepared.
Gaily the lights through Arch and Oriel streamed;
Their blazonry in richest colours gleamed.
Amid the trophies which with festive grace
Adorned the Tables and o'erhung the Dais,
An Emblem chiefly challenging the sight —
Was that famed Triple Plume of purest white,
Edward of Woodstock's, — won on Crécy's plain
From John, Bohemia's King, — in battle slain. [2]

[1] Henry Mordaunt, a Lieutenant in the 46th Regiment, was the third and youngest son of the late Rev. Charles Mordaunt of Gatcombe Court, Rector of Badgworth, Somerset, and cousin of the late Sir Charles Mordaunt, Bart. These young men were attached by the strongest ties of mutual friendship, and Henry Mordaunt, it is feared, lost his life by accepting, on his arrival with the 46th from Gibraltar, the offer of Eustace d'Eyncourt, who had already landed from England, to share his quarters. When, six days afterwards, (4th March, 1842,) Eustace was seized by the Yellow Fever, Henry carefully nursed and sat up all night with him. On the second day he was himself attacked. While lying in adjoining rooms, they reciprocated the most affectionate enquiries. Eustace expired on the 9th. Henry, when informed of his friend's departure, uttered an exclamation of deep feeling, — never spoke afterwards, and died in the same evening. Colonel Garrett of the 46th thus speaks of them, in May 1842, in a letter to Henry Mordaunt's brother: — "They were two as noble, manly, kind-hearted and generous beings as ever breathed; and it will be very —very long before the Regiment will recover from the gloom cast over it by the loss of such friends and companions as these departed young men." Major Maxwell of the 46th, in a letter to another relation of Henry Mordaunt, says: — "The friends were buried next day side by side in the same grave, deeply and sincerely regretted by every person in the Regiment, officers and men, leaving a blank behind them which will never be filled up." The officers of the 46th erected a handsome tomb over their grave, with an inscription to their memory. Henry Mordaunt was 23 years of age, and his noble spirit is sufficiently evidenced by the fact, that while at Gibraltar he saved the lives of two men, at the imminent peril of his own, by swimming from Europa Point, when no other person would venture in a boat or otherwise, on account of the extreme roughness of the sea. It is needless to add that he was deeply loved and lamented by his widowed mother and family.

[2] The long existing doubt and controversy with regard to the origin of the Plume borne by Edward the Black Prince, and subsequently by Male Heirs to the Throne, appears to be set at rest by a paper recently (May 1847) contributed by Sir Harris Nicholas to the

# EUSTACE; AN ELEGY

The Crown and Crest, with Motto quaint entwined,
For this festivity a cause assigned: —
The Heir of England, on that day, received[1]
The Holy Sign, in Christendom believed
A Rite, all inborn Evil to destroy,
Imparting Grace to win Eternal Joy.

"ALBERT, — to Thee, — may such the symbol prove!
"Long may the Royal Line retain the Love
"Which Christian Princes only can acquire,
"Which Christian Virtues can alone inspire!"

Such was the Shout which filled the lofty Hall,
Which shook the beaming armour on its wall,
And waved the Banners from its rafters hung:
Along the Roof responding music rung,
While All, with Heart and Voice the Loyal Anthem sung.

Thy fervent accents, Eustace, swelled the Strain; —
No Heart, than Thine, more Valiant to maintain
The Race, by Freemen, placed upon the Throne,
To guard the Rights their Ancestors had won.

But not for this alone the Board was spread: —
A soft domestic feeling also led
His Parents thus to call their friend around,
To bid Farewell to Eustace, who was bound
On distant Service to that fated Isle,
Their sorrow so to hide — if not beguile;
To dress the last Adieus in colours gay,
And leave him, when on Duty, far away,
A sweet remembrance of the latest hours
He spent within his dear paternal Towers.
It is such household scenes as these which form
The memoried World of Youth; — the later Charm, —

Society of Antiquaries (See *Archæologia*, vol. xxxii, p.332), wherein he refers to the contemporary authority of John de Ardern, a celebrated physician in the court of Edward III, who in a work, two copies of which are to be found in the Sloane Collection (No. 56, fo. 76, and 335, fo. 67), distinctly confirms the popular opinion, that having been borne as the crest of the King of Bohemia when slain at Crécy, it was thenceforth adopted by Prince Edward, the hero of that battle, designated by Ardern when he records his death in 1376, as "*Flos militæ mundi — sine pare.*"

[1] His Royal Highness, Albert Edward, Prince of Wales, was baptised at Windsor on 25th January, 1842.

Which, through the Cares and Griefs of riper Age,
Gilds with a sacred Light the early page
Of that poor History, — Man's Pilgrimage!

He was the Life — the Spirit of the scene: —
But there were moments, when a pause between
The varied pleasures of the Evening came, —
The light which from his Eye was wont to beam,
Seemed on a sudden, dim; — as if a thought —
Or latent consciousness of ill, had brought
Some deep reflection which his Heart oppressed, —
Some sad conviction which his Soul confessed:
Yet, when the Music had the Dance renewed,
Again, with sympathetic warmth indued,
Joining the throng, he, — gayest of the gay,
In sport and mirth seductive, led the way.

———

A second banquet, after midnight, cheered
The lively revellers till morn appeared;
And if, from time to time, a gloom were cast
Upon his gentle brow, — it quickly passed.
A manly effort seemed to give him power
To banish thoughts unsuited to the hour.
His playful arts to please the Guests around, —
His brilliant sallies, — made the Hall resound
With peals of laughter: — Yet, — unbidden came
A Spectral phantasm — an uneasy dream, —
A dismal presage, forced upon his mind —
A painful feeling — dark and undefined —
That this bright scene, no more, his eyes would view:
That thence — for ever — he must bid adieu
To Home and Parents — Brothers, Sisters, Friends! —
But so the thought with sportive feeling blends,
That these, conspiring, caused a strange conceit
To strike his fancy. — Rising from his seat
He left the Hall, — appearing as he went,
As if, to greet some Guest, his steps were bent.

And soon, — a Stranger at the Board appeared, —
In garb antique arrayed — with grisly beard; —
An aged man, whose lofty bearing shewed
His title to respect and Noble blood.

"I come," he said, "to share in all your joy, —
"For at Old Bayons oft — as man and boy,
"In antient times, have I the revel joined,
"When Lord, and Knight, and Vassal, — all combined,
"Would thus assemble here in festive State,
"Some great Event to mark and celebrate."

A whisper rose: — but eager, all, to spell
The mystic words which from the Stranger fell.
He thus proceeded with a cheerful grace
And brilliant eye, — tho' motionless his face:

"Edward the Third his time, (whose Image there
"Still glads my sight), saw me in blither cheer
"Than now to you, most likely, I appear.
"Five centuries within my neighbouring Tomb,
"(Whereon, just now, I read my earthly doom)
"I slept in peace; — when suddenly, — a Shout
"Struck my dull ear and roused my slumbering thought.
"It was a Cheer to warm my English heart,
"And new-born vigor to my limbs impart.
"I broke my bonds, — and passing onward, found
"The cause of that enlivening, joyous sound
"Which called me forth, and guided me to join
"Your gathering here to bless VICTORIA'S Line.

"Of Old, we much affected Feasts like these,
"Where sat together men of all degrees,
"Stirring their natures to a generous zeal
"For any cause which touched the Public Weal;
"They woke the Spirit which our Victories gained
"At Crécy — Durham — Poictiers: — and sustained
"Our noble Monarch and his Gallant Son,
"In fifty battles by their prowess won.
"'Twas thus we learned with courage to defend
"King, Law, Hearth, Altar, Lady-love or Friend.

"And now, my Soul rejoices to behold
"A Harvest from the seed we sowed of Old.
"The Antient Laws of England we maintained;
"The Sovereign loved — but by those Laws restrained.
"VICTORIA, — scion of King Edward's race —
"Now occupies, I learn, his Royal place;
"With Virtue — Beauty — Gentleness, combined, —

"With every attribute of Heart and Mind
"To warm your Loyalty and guide the State, —
"Blessings, which ages have matured, await
"This goodly Realm, if you are staunch and true
"To those Old Maxims which, of yore, I knew: —
"*Maintain the People's Rights — The Queen defend —*
"*Obey the Laws — To God your Soul commend.*'

  "With you — I hail the advent of an Heir
"To England's Throne: — with you — the hope I share,
"The Great — and Good — and Wise — he may become
"(Like him who conquered that Immortal Plume)
"The People's Hope — his Country's Pride and Grace —
"The Star and Glory of his Royal Race.
"That honoured Emblem is a sacred Trust!
"May Albert live to prove his Title just
"To bear The Plume which decked a Hero's head,
"By learning in our Edward's Path to tread: —
"That Noblest Knight who e'er the World adorned!
"By all the Chivalry of Europe mourned,
"When Heaven, impatient for so dear a prize,
"Gave him a Crown, eternal, in the Skies.
"His Valour, Virtue, gentleness and worth,
"This Princely Infant claims by right of birth;
"And so he adds to 'Albert' — Edward's name,
"So may he add to Edward's — Albert's fame.
"But yet unlike him in his early fate,
"May He survive, in Peace, to rule the State,
"When Queen Victoria, after glorious years,
"Shall pass away, amidst a nation's tears! —
"For Her, — I pray, that She may thus be spared
"The bitter grief which my King Edward shared
"With many a Father, whom, his battles won
"Left to deplore the loss of some dear Son,
"Who seeking glory by his Valour earned,
"*To Home and Parents never more returned.*"

  The Stranger paused, as if oppressed by thought: —
His Eye — the Manor's Lord and Lady sought; —
Then thus, — in tones with tenderest feeling fraught: —

  "May all the choicest Gifts which Heaven hath stored,
"On Those who here preside, be richly poured.
"On Them — for reasons which my Heart avows, —

"Such blessings rare, my parting Voice bestows; —
"Blessings which you will aid me to invoke."

   The Company arose, when thus bespoke,
To join in rendering all the honours due; —
But still, with varying doubts, the Stranger view.

   "My Friends," he said, "long since the Clock struck *ONE!*
"A Spirit whispers in my Ear, — 'Begone!'
"Bound by a Law — imperative and stern,
"Unto my lowly bed I must return,
"And Converse with the Upper World forego,
"Ere morning Light appears — or Cock shall crow!
"But when, hereafter, you assemble here
"On some occasion such as this, — I swear —
"That if again your Shout the Dead shall wake,
"I will appear amongst you, and partake
"Your Joy, if not your Cheer: — till then, Farewell!"

   He turned away: — but some mischance befel
The wrinkled mask which had his face concealed —
And Eustace d'Eyncourt's features stood revealed!

   The doubting Guests resumed their mirth and glee,
Their Friend and Favorite in this guise to see.
But yet, in these his Father scarcely joined; —
Deep feeling seemed to agitate his mind.
At length he rose, and, with emotion, said:

   "May this dear Son, so risen from the Dead,
"Now long remain to justify, on Earth,
"The hope his Parents cherished from his birth,
"That he, the pride of their Old Age would be,
"And bring high Honour to his Family.
"To-morrow's Sun will light him on his way
"To serve the Queen in Countries far away; —
"Years may elapse before again we meet!
"May You be here his safe return to greet!
"Aid me to tell him with your general voice,
"How all of you, with me, will then rejoice
"To see again within his Father's Hall,
"The Son — of whom no act can I recal,
"Or transient word, — or look — which could offend
"His Father's feelings, or his Father's friend:

"May heaven bless him!"
                                    Here the loud acclaim
Made the high Chamber echo with his name.

  Altho' by all beloved, admired, esteemed, —
Yet, as his modest nature had not deemed
That warmth, like this, would hail his youthful name, —
Deeply he blushed from that high minded shame,
Which those, unconsciously by virtue graced,
Feel at the praise they fear may be misplaced.
But still, a quick response of grateful joy
Aroused the impulse sparkling in his eye,
When, in his touching tones, he thus expressed
The mingled feelings which his heart oppressed.

  "Friends of my youth! how shall my breast disclose
"The grateful sentiment with which it glows?
"There is no Human language to impart
"The sweet mysterious movements of the Heart.
"Words are the signs which usual thoughts express:
"But for the feelings which our bosoms bless
"When deep emotions, never felt before,
"By some electric, instantaneous power,
"Surprise our Souls, — the tongue will strive in vain
"The new, unknown sensation to explain.
"I long to shew — but language is denied, —
"How dear my Home and Friends; and what the pride, —
"With which, in lonely hours, beyond the Sea, —
"Musing on this fair scene and Company, —
"I shall recall that warm and thrilling Cheer,
"Which, — while I live, — will this short hour endear.
"Such Memories, — like distant Music, — come
"To sooth our Cares when far away from home.
"They are the golden links, by mercy, placed
"Between the gloomy present and the Past;
"The charms they yield, our energies sustain,
"When worn by irksome toil, by grief or pain; —
"For then — our thoughts recur to distant friends, —
"Repose on Pictures, which our Memory lends,
"Of dear domestic Scenes; — and thus we find
"Reflected from that Mirror of the Mind,
"Soft gleams of Hope that patience may subdue
"Our present ills, and such delights renew.
"And from the Memory of this Night will spring

106

Figure 12: Eustace Tennyson d'Eyncourt addressing the company assembled in the Great Hall of Bayons Manor, January 1842. Lithograph by Dickinson and Co. for Charles Tennyson d'Eyncourt's *Eustace (1851)*.

"My firm resolve that, some day, I will bring
"A better title to the kind applause,
"Your generous feeling now alone bestows.
"My fond remembrance of the tenderest ties
"Which give the Charm to human destinies: —
"Friendship and filial love, — or, let me say
"To those bright Beings here around, that they —
"And all the sweet illusions they inspire, —
"Will, in my breast, awake the proud desire
"To prove, — if called my Country to defend
"In Battle-Field, — that I, your youthful friend,
"Am not unworthy of the Name I bear, —
"A Parent's blessing, — or a Lady's prayer.


   "But if, — by Heaven's decree, I come no more!
"May it accept the Prayers my heart would pour
"For You who cheer me in this parting hour.
"The Golden Cup from which I drink to You,
"While I pronounce, with pain, my last Adieu, —
"May, when you see it grace my Father's board,
"Sometimes remind you of my latest word, —
"Which, though of joy to me, it seems the knell,
"For You, bespeaks it in that word — *Farewell!*"


   He ceased. A deep responsive feeling moved
Their swelling bosoms for the Youth beloved: —
While he, behind his Parents' seat retired.
His Father, then, a gentle thought inspired; —
And as of general Converse rose the tide,
He turned, and called the Soldier to his side.
Holding the Golden Chalice in his hand, —
"My Son," he said, — "No need this Cup should stand
"Before *our* Eyes in memory of *Thee!*
"Thy Image in our Hearts will ever be:
"Bear it away in memory of *Me!*
"And in those social hours — with pleasant friends,
"When cheerful converse anxious thought unbends, —
"If they discourse upon thy native land —
"Of Home — and homely things, — this Cup at hand,
"Charged with a tribute to such early ties,
"More surely will awake thy sympathies.
"It may remind thee of thy Parents' Hearth, —
"Of those who loved thee, Eustace, from thy birth: —
"Yes, — still more sweetly will thy heart respond,

# EUSTACE; AN ELEGY

"When this, — thy Father's Cup, — shall pass around."

While deep emotion crimsoned o'er his cheek,
The Soldier, — for a moment, — paused to seek
Such words as to his Father might convey
All that his Heart, — if it could speak, — would say.
Striving, in vain, his quivering Lip to hide,
At length he took the Chalice, — and replied:

"Not as a *Gift*, — would I, from thy dear hand,
"Receive the Cup I take by thy command; —
"Remaining thine, I feel that it may prove
"A sweeter gage of thy paternal love
"Than if a Gift, — and so transferred to me,
"The link were gone connecting it with thee.
"Having, for years, by thee been known and used,
"Into its Form, my fancy has infused
"A lingering Charm or Instinct, — which will seem
"To spring from Thee, — and haply I may dream
"When clasping it, that by some mystic power
"We hold communion: — even, that this Hour,
"When I receive thy blessing on my head,
"Is still prolonged — and not for ever fled!
"Thus let me keep it — till I cease to be
"What now I am and feel, — a Son to Thee!"

"Such thou wilt ever be" the Father said,
"And so 'tis Thine!" — The Father had not read
The hidden meaning in his Son's reply,
Which shadowed forth a fearful prophecy;
But simply added, — "When thy sorrows come, —
"(For such, on Earth, are man's allotted doom)
"This may recal the Friend who cannot fail,
"If sympathy or aid can aught avail, —
"The Friend whom Nature to a Child hath given, —
"His surest help and comfort under Heaven!"

Their hands' warm pressure, and their eyes, declare
The deep affection which their bosoms share:
And if a filial tear the compact sealed
And mixed with those, from purest love distilled,
With which a Parent had the Cup bedewed, —
Such holy union thus the Pledge imbued
With Power more sacred to confirm a Bond,

Which Nature sanctioned and their hearts had owned.

———

The Night, — with all its changing scenes — was past! —
That morning came — decreed to be the last,
When this dear Son would see the Orb of day
Smile on his Home, and deck in bright array
The varied Landscape from his casement viewed,
Which all the Memories of his Youth renewed.

Then came the parting hour! — the long caress!
The deep — fond look, which more than words — can bless:
Sweetly, — a Mother's clinging Arms enfold
His Manly Form, — and so her Sorrow told. —
Her whispered Orison to Heaven addressed,
His last Embrace which held her to his breast,
His lingering kiss of reverential Love,—
The sacred sadness of their bosoms prove.
He moved away: — and then — o'erwhelmed by grief,
He felt that utterance might afford relief. —
His steps returned: — once more — his eyes surveyed
The weeping group: at length his voice obeyed
The impulse deepest sorrow ever feels: —
A simple Prayer his latest thought reveals:

"May God for ever bless you all," he cried:
A smile angelic seemed his tears to chide, —
Pictured the bliss his Spirit would invoke,
And left the healing balm his soul bespoke.

———

\* \* \* \* \* \*

In twice Twelve days had Eustace passed the Sea:
Another Twelve, — and he had ceased to be!
But 'ere in Death his languid eyes were closed,
Their fading Vision on the Cup reposed: —
A dying Sign, — more sacred than Command, —
Bequeathed it Homeward with his faltering hand.
This pious thought fulfilled — this act of Love, —
His spirit winged its way to Realms above! —

The Chalice — silent witness to his Will, —
Had then a mournful mission to fulfil.
Dulled by the damps which in that Chamber fell,

110

The Golden Herald came its tale to tell. —
But as, from Heaven, a Chastening Angel brings,
With Evil tidings, healing on his Wings,
That tale of Sorrow, so with Love combined,
Diffused a holy influence o'er the mind,
And left it Calm, Submissive, and Resigned.
*Resigned* to ills, which in this mortal state
Are born of Blessings, when withdrawn by Fate;
Yet, — grateful that such Gifts from Mercy's Store
*Had* blessed existence — though they blessed no more;
*Submissive* to receive both Good and Ill,
As each is dealt by God's unerring Will:
Conscious that Human Reason must not scan
The Laws — unknown — which guide His Ways to Man:
That seeming Ills, may haply, Blessings prove,
Fruit of His Mercy and enduring Love.

Thus, from Affliction, deeper thoughts arise, —
And Man is taught by Sorrow — to be Wise.
And if from Wisdom, nobler Virtues spring, —
If nobler Virtues, higher Bliss shall bring, —
Who may presume to question GOD'S decree,
Or deem his chastisements, — Adversity!

———

The Farewell Cup to Bayons Hall restored,
Now stands apart — and Sacred — on the Board; —
Fulfils the Soldier's wish when it renews
A sweet remembrance of his last Adieus; —
Recals his fond and dying thought of Home,
And forms a link with EUSTACE — in the Tomb.

## CANTO III

----

*"Moneat quoque — quam fugaces!*
*Quantula sit Vita!"*

----

THINK! — What is Life! — a wandering irksome dream! —
A vain pursuit of some imperfect scheme! —
All that you know of human Life — is gone!
You lived just now — and may, you think — live on.
But how! — or where! — and when! — do you exist? —
This, from your sight, is hidden by the mist
Which mercifully veils from Mortals here,
Truths that their Senses are unfit to bear.

Where ends the *Past — the Future* must begin: —
You live in neither, — but sustained between,
Your Being — a point in visionary space,
To which can be assigned — nor Time nor Place, —
Is ever gliding on, — until at last, —
Your *lessening Future — all* becomes the *Past!*

*Thy* Being, O GOD, the Past and Future fills!
Throughout the Universe Thy Spirit thrills.
Thou seest, o'er Things of Time, the Ages flow,
As One, — Eternal, — comprehensive 'NOW'!

But Man's frail Being every instant dies:
His vapid thought from past to Future flies; —
Such Knowledge only as Sensation brings
In that swift passage on Electric Wings,
Inspires his Clay and *to the Spirit clings.*
His Consciousness of this mysterious tie
Connecting Past and Future, — 'Memory,' —
Is all the '*Present*' he can here enjoy.

112

# EUSTACE; AN ELEGY

Without a *Real* 'Present' where the Soul
Might all it's force concentre and control,
Man's *past* impressions form his scanty Lore
On Life's tempestuous, ever varying Shore, —
Where, all before him, is a fearful Sea
Of measureless — untried Futurity, —
And all the Past, a troubled region seems
Of ill-remembered — evanescent dreams.

From these, he seeks in vain some latent Sign
To indicate, of Life, the Laws divine, —
Some revelation of a heavenly Power
To solve the mysteries of that shifting Shore: —
But how can Memory's Shadows flitting there,
In feeble whisperings of the *Past*, declare
The Secret which sustains the Vital flame
In Beings ever changing — yet the same!

Such is that fitful Trance — the Life of Man!
But at his Waking! — then — the wondrous plan
Of Life and Death, Eternity and Time,
May be unfolded, — with the Truths Sublime
Which Good and Evil, Right and Wrong, compel
To work together by some mighty spell,
And so the warring principles control
That perfect Harmony pervades the Whole.

These Mysteries — from human sight concealed,
May to your purer Spirit be revealed.
But mark! — that henceforth you must well prepare
Your Soul such High Intelligence to Share.
Vast and ennobling are the Powers bestowed
On Man while here below; — with these endowed
You have at your command a Rich Domain:
On *You* depends the Harvest you obtain.
The thoughtless Tenant may refuse to toil
And loathsome weeds will desolate the soil.
Seduced by vain and transitory joys,
For these he barters an Eternal Prize.
The Phantom, — Pleasure, — eagerly pursued,
Invites its Victim only to delude:
The instant you approach, it disappears, —
Or some distorted form its head uprears.
You grasp at Shadows, — or your fate is worse, —

113

The Bliss your fancy whispered — proves a Curse!

Yet, of the Blessings Providence prepares
To soothe your passage through this World of Cares,
Freely partake: — 'tis God's benignant plan
To smooth the rudeness of his path to Man.
But when the Cup of Pleasure passes round,
Drink not too deeply, for below, are found
The bitter dregs which poison Moral Sense, —
The Power provided for your Soul's defence.
Affliction may correct the human mind,
Render it humble, pious, and resigned;
But Pleasure, unrestrained, *itself* destroys, —
Consumes all sensibility to joys, —
And leaves its Votary, impure, debased,
His Heart corrupted, and his Mind, — a Waste.
Pleasures are Blessings to the Good and Wise.
Curses to those who all restraint despise.
Such Blessings, therefore, moderately use:
All gratefully accept — nor aught abuse.
The Golden precept for your guidance here
Is simply this: — *'In all things to Forbear.'*
Virtue herself this Maxim must obey: —
Excesses — even Virtue's cause betray.
Add to Forbearance, — earnest — useful Toil;
For idle habits, heart and mind despoil
Of moral power: — and this the right will give
The fruits of labour to partake, — and Live.
Encrease the Public Wealth, or Wisdom's store,
And grateful for Existence, — GOD adore!

This is Contentment! — such is the device,
Whereby to win the only Pearl of Price!
The Gem Philosophers have sought in vain:
Th' Elixir to subdue all moral pain! —
The Alchemists — to Truth and Ethics blind,
Tortured the Elements of Earth to find
A source of boundless Wealth, — the Magic Wand,
All worldly Pleasures freely to command, —
The Toil of others to control at will,
And every dream of Power and Pride fulfil.

Vain thought! — that boundless Wealth could supersede
The Laws for Man's well-being by heaven decreed!

114

His Happiness on Earth alone depends
On HOPE, — and all the Energy it lends
To gain by Labour, Care, and anxious Thought,
Ends — only valued when by Labour sought.
But if the objects Man should so attain,
The Talisman of Wealth, or Power, can gain, —
Then HOPE — the twin-born Sister of DESIRE,
No more, by cheering whispers, will inspire
Efforts to reach the fruit they cease to prize,
But droops at once — and with her Sister dies.
A mocking Fiend usurps her vacant seat —
Pretends that heaven is false, and Life a Cheat;
His Victim counsels, Virtue to forswear,
And in a Sea of vice to drown DESPAIR.

But GOD is Just — supremely Good and Wise, —
Though such the fate of Man's Idolatries;
And Life *has* Blessings to reward the toil
Of those who seek their course to reconcile
With Nature's Laws — immutable — Divine —
Which Human Bliss with Usefulness combine.

Superfluous Wealth, a cause of constant strife,
Disturbs, by stormy Cares, the Stream of Life.
They are the Rich, who have delights in Store:
Those who exhaust them are the truly Poor:
That Man is blest who governs his desires, —
Extends to All, th' indulgence *he* requires;
Relieves the wants of others where he can,
And serves his GOD by doing good to Man.
No other Alchemy you need but this,
To bring you Peace on Earth, and Heavenly Bliss,
A sense of which may even here begin:

There is a Power Ethereal dwells within
Your Mortal part, while yet on earth detained,
Whereby th' immortal Spirit is sustained,
When it shall seek to soar beyond the Skies —
And thus — entranced, — to purer regions rise.
The Spirit is of God, — with his combined;
Part of the vast Intelligence which reigned
Throughout the Universe 'ere yet began
The Earthly Race in which it dwells as *Man*.

This deathless Spirit which informs the Clay,
Imparts a Power the Dictates to obey
Of Love Divine — on Truth-Eternal based —
And on the Heart of Man, in mercy, traced.
Man feels them to be Holy, Just and Wise,
E'en when his Life their influence defies.
However steeped in Vice or lost to shame,
He honours Virtue while he dreads her name.
The Spirit's Light is ever on his Soul,
Although his Passions may resist control.
Passions are Powers intended to be used;
But Crime results from those just Powers abused.
*Rightly* to use them, for the Ends designed,
Is the great task allotted to Mankind.
Wherefore, a Heavenly Light hath been bestowed
To guide the Earthly Pilgrim on his Road,
Through this dark Region, to a bright Abode.
Though Nature's secrets be from Man concealed,
As needless for his State to be revealed: —
Although the object of his brief career,
And all the Mystery of his presence here,
Be deeply veiled, — The Spirit hath inspired
A Moral Sense by Social Man required.
Thus far — the Will of God hath been expressed
By Laws recorded in the human breast.
Therein exists a Court o'er which presides
A Monitor, whose glorious Wisdom guides
All who shall humbly seek this Heavenly Light
Their thoughts and actions to direct aright.
That Monitor is *Conscience*, — ever True: —
And Conscience, — What? — *The Voice of GOD in You!*

So will your Passions curbed, your Thoughts refined,
Expand your Heart and elevate your Mind.
Your Nature purified, — will then aspire
To Realms Sublime! — then will your Soul desire
With Essences Divine to commune there,
Their Wisdom and Beatitude to share.

# EUSTACE; AN ELEGY

## Invocation

Lamented EUSTACE ! I invoke thy Shade
These moral Truths, — this warning Voice to aid.

With genius, energy, and Power of Mind,
Beyond the usual fortune of Mankind:
Exempt from Passions which the heart deprave:
Forbearing, constant, generous and brave;
Gentle, but firm, benevolent and true, —
Would that my Summons could thy Life renew!

But yet — thy Memory loved — thy death deplored —
The varied Excellence thy Soul had stored —
Inspire a hope — that in some radiant Clime,
Freed from the sorrows and the bonds of Time, —
Immortal — Happy — full of Glorious Grace,
Thy Angel-Spirit watches o'er thy Race.

As Each, in turn, shall pass beyond the Pale
Of Death and Sin, — may thy bright Presence hail
Their Advent! —
                    First, behold! thy Parents come; —
Doubting and fearful, — they await their Doom!

Ah, then! — if Earthly Love, so pure as thine,
Survive to mix the Elements Divine, —
Approach them with that fond effulgent smile,
Which here, so often, would their cares beguile: —
Their humble Spirits cheer, and lead them on,
To kneel with thee before Th' Eternal Throne.

*Note:*
Apart from the early "A perfectly New Chorus..." written jointly with George, no other work by Charles has been included in this edition of the poems by the two Tennyson brothers. Two lines attributed to Charles (and a version of the same by Old George) are printed in *Memoir*, I, p.13. There exists at L.A.O. two poems in Charles's hand: "The King of the Cannibal Islands" and "Meet me by Moonlight" (T.d'E. H163/21). The paper is watermarked 'G. H. GREEN / 1830'. It is impossible to determine if they are Charles's work: they have the feel of the light verse which may have been recited at the family entertainments and theatricals, popular at Bayons in the late 1830s (see L.A.O. 2 T.d'E. H64/49), and as such may be copies of the work of other, as yet unidentified, versifiers. L.A.O. calendars 2T.d'E. H17/2 as 'Poems, after Burns (by Charles T[ennyson]?)'. The manuscript is endorsed 'Brancepeth'. Although Charles made some alterations to the manuscript, most of it appears to be in Fanny's hand. L.A.O. T.d'E

H152/1, "On an Annual Dinner Given at Winchester College", is also (erroneously) attributed to Charles.

An observation offered by Elizabeth Russell in September 1815, made apropos Charles's letters from Paris, is appropriate here: 'There is *something* in *everything* you write from a law paper to a flight of fancy, which gratifies and charms me; your minuteness is never tedious because it is penned with vivacity and purity which carries with it the force of truth, and if you were to tell me that in France the men had green hair, and that the women wore whiskers I should be inclined to believe you, but I so rarely have a line from you, that I live upon the fruits of your former genius, of which I possess more than you guess, having some of your school productions, commonly called themes, which are interlined something like the M.S. of Pope's Homer....' (L.A.O. T.d'E. H 73/4).

*Other Publications:*
The following list of Charles's political pamphlets and antiquarian articles makes no claim to bibliographical completeness. No attempt has been made to search the more ephemeral material relating to elections, nor the literature of the masonic movement in which Charles was deeply involved - for the latter see especially R. S. E. Sandbach, *Priest and Freemason: the Life of George Oliver* (London, 1988).

*Observations on the Proceedings Against the Queen [Caroline], Addressed to his Constituents...* (London, 1821).

*Report of Speech... on Seconding Mr. John Smith's Motion for the Restoration of the Queen's Name to the Liturgy* (London, 1821).

*Report of Speech... on moving the Second Reading of the Bill for the Prohibiting the Use of Spring Guns* (London, 1825).

*Speech... on Mr. N. Calvert's Motion to Substitute the Hundred of Bassetlaw for the Town of Birmingham in the... Bill for Disfranchising... East Retford* (London, [1828]).

*Repeal of the Septennial Act. Speech... on Moving for a Bill to Shorten the Duration of Parliaments...* (London, 1834).

'Memoir on the leaden plate, the memorial of William d'Eyncourt, preserved in the cathedral library, at Lincoln', *Memoir Illustrative of the History and Antiquities of the County and City of Lincoln, Communicated to the Annual Meeting of the Archaeological Institute of Great Britain and Ireland, Held at Lincoln, July 1848* (London, 1850), pp.248-52 [included in J. B. Burke's *Memorials of Bayons Manor...* (1852)].

'Notice of a portrait of John, King of France', *Archaeologia*, XXXVIII (1860), pp.196-201.

# INFLUENCE ON ALFRED TENNYSON

The life and writings of Dr George Clayton Tennyson are of interest in themselves but obviously acquire extra significance because of their effect on the work of his famous son. The fear of epilepsy which haunted Alfred, as well as the bouts of melancholia to which he was susceptible,[1] can both be attributed to his close identification with his difficult and over-bearing father, who was his tutor during the crucial years between 1820, when he left school in Louth, and 1827, when he went up to Cambridge. The tuition was increasingly broken by the rector's illnesses and the introspective adolescent was inevitably drawn into his father's dark and troubled world, a world which much later was delineated in some of his greatest poems, notably *Maud*. Robert Bernard Martin suggests that 'Alfred kept his sympathy for his father alive in a way most unusual for a boy of his age put in such an intolerable environment.'[2] A letter to his uncle, written at the age of sixteen, reveals the extent of that sympathy:

> My dear Uncle
> It is with great sorrow that I inform you that my poor father is not any better than before. He had another violent attack of the same nature yesterday. Indeed no one but those who are continually with him can conceive what he suffers, as he is never entirely free from this alarming illness. He is reduced to such a degree of weakness from these repeated attacks, that the slightest shock is sufficient to bring them on again. Perhaps if he could summon resolution enough to get out more, he would be relieved, but the lassitude which the fits leave incapacitates him from undergoing any exertion. He has already had two of these since my grandfather was here which is not much more than a week ago & some time previous to that had three each night successively. He was not able to attend the Bishop's Visitation on Friday. With kindest remembrances to my aunt & cousins
>
> Believe me, my dear Uncle,<br>Yours affectionately<br>A Tennyson[3]

When he was eighteen and about to go to Cambridge, Alfred could no longer bear the pain of watching his father's suffering. He was driven to staying at the hated Bayons with his grandfather; when he heard that his uncle Charles planned to bring his father there too, he fled to Cambridge and at last to a new life[4] - but his early

---

[1]   See also Jack Kolb's review article 'Portraits of Tennyson', *Modern Philology*, 81, 2 (November 1983), pp.173-90 for a criticism of the accepted notion of the 'black blood' of the Tennysons as presented by Martin. For more on the medical background to the family's epilepsy in relation to Alfred's work, see Barbara Herb Wright 'Tennyson, the weird seizures in *The Princess*, and epilepsy', *Literature and Medicine*, 6 (1987), pp.61-76.

[2]   Martin, p.39.

[3]   L.A.O. T.d'E. H147/4 (*Letters A.T.*, I, p.6), [2 August 1825].

[4]   In July 1830, when Dr Tennyson was about to return to Lincolnshire, Alfred fled, on the pretext of consulting a physician, to London, whence he travelled to the Pyrenees with Hallam.

intense exposure to his father's black moods left its mark ever afterwards, both on his life and on his work.

George Clayton Tennyson's poems have therefore an interest beyond the purely biographical. Alfred was always an eager performer of his own work, delighting in an audience. It seems very likely that he had heard his father's poems similarly declaimed during the lonely years at Somersby. When he and his brother Charles had their *Poems by Two Brothers* published in 1827, they drove to the sea at Mablethorpe and shouted snatches of their poetry to the waves. Declamation was of the essence of their poetic talent: when he was only seven and about to go to Louth School, Alfred had been made by his father to recite Horace's *Odes* by heart.[1] He could probably have recited his father's verse from memory too - and he did write out a version of George's "Mad Tom". His admiration for his father's work was more than mere filial piety. 'My father was a poet,' he told his son, Hallam, 'and could write regular metre very skilfully'. He recalled his father's early advice: 'Don't write so rhythmically, break your lines occasionally for the sake of variety.'[2]

Dr Tennyson failed to follow his own advice. His verse is metrically unadventurous, full of imitations of the poets whose works were to be found in the Rectory library.[3] However, a first group of poems, all exercises in eighteenth century wit, have energy, charm and vivacity and hint poignantly at the 'noble mind o'erthrown' by the Doctor's later troubles. "A Perfectly New Chorus..." was written with Charles ('the Clerk and Advocate') and addressed to Elizabeth Russell, their 'beloved sister in the North'. In this poem they ruefully contrast their sister's imagined life of ease at Hardwicke with their own diurnal struggle for existence. The rhythmical challenge they have set themselves is like a school exercise (George, it will be recalled, was noted during his schooldays for writing verse in answer to questions set). Sibling rivalry is here turned into affectionate playfulness. There is however something precarious in the structure of the poem. Later in life, away from Elizabeth's benign influence, both brothers fell into a crippling seriousness, and in George's case into melancholy. "A Tribute to the Memory of Mr Leander ———" is an example of George's lighthearted wit - a wit evident in his letters to his brother, but sadly fading from his life by the 1820s.

"A Sublime Ode in Two Parts on Wintry Weather" can be dated more accurately than the other poems. It deals satirically with the Prince of Wales's attempts to humiliate his wife, later Queen Caroline, and therefore must have been written at the height of the controversy in c.1806. (The affair moved many writers, notably Coleridge, to take up arms in favour of the victimised queen.) The tone is

---

1  'Tennyson's father', p.300 (but note also Paden, p. 101).
2  *Memoir*, I, pp.11-12.
3  The inventory of Dr Tennyson's library drawn up in 1831 (T.R.C.) lists works by some twenty-five authors, including Spenser (the 1590 edition of *The Faerie Queen* - the volume is at T.R.C.), Milton, Dryden's Virgil (1697), Thomson, Cowper, 'Ossian', Rogers, Scott and Byron. He also owned Sir William Jones's works in 6 volumes (London, 1799) which contains the poems.

vigorous and coarse and smacks more of the eighteenth than the nineteenth century. The wit lies in the rigorous adherence to the satirical metre, the outrageous rhymes ('ducal/puke all' etc.) and the most unclerical irreverence. George's letters to his brother reveal a similar earthiness, suppressed beneath the weight of his later troubles. It is difficult to find in his son's poetry anything approaching such coarseness: George is ultimately a man of the Regency period. Only in his attack on Bulwer-Lytton in "The New Timon, and the Poets" in 1846 does Alfred approach anything like such invective.

A second group of poems exploits a vein of elegiac wistfulness and is centred on the figure of Elizabeth Russell as Muse. The "Verses Addressed to a Lady on Her Departure" were obviously one of the Doctor's own favourites: he copied them out much later for his adored niece, Julia. Elizabeth Russell is surely the 'Star of the North' whose departure brings him such sadness. Behind the conventional Pre-Romantic images lies real feeling. The verse form - three iambic pentameters followed by an iambic trimeter, with an abba rhyme scheme - allows the last line of each verse to melt away into regret. This is the world of the lonely adolescent, in which imagination supersedes reality and memory becomes a luxurious pain. The eighteenth-century Wit is now the pensive elegist, versed in Gray and Thomson. Sensual pleasure is rejected in favour of the spiritual. "The Minstrel's Lament" and "Unsullied Album" share the prevailing mood and all give an insight into the poetic climate upon which, in 1798, burst Wordsworth and Coleridge's *Lyrical Ballads*. George's enervated imagery ('thy dreary pomp', 'refulgent fire', 'the gloomy vault of night') suggests insufficient energy for the task he adumbrates - that of finding an authentic new voice, 'on native pinions born'; his third son was to do much better.

A third group of poems - heavily annotated and reworked, and probably dating from later in Dr Tennyson's life - are Spenserian stanzas dealing with flight from nameless threat and full of gloomy philosophising on the transience of life. In "The Wandering Jew" George finds his ideal persona: the guilt-ridden exile, condemned to wander the world, friendless and self-tormenting. The 'incidents so horrible and rare' might well simply relate to the writer's rich fantasy life. The early Russian adventure (1801/2) would certainly have allowed him to play at being the Wandering Jew and the sad flight across the Continent shortly before his death seems strangely prefigured here too. Exotic settings, like those of Alfred's early poetry, are really landscapes of the mind and the poems are largely fragments. The central one, the subject of George's obsessive attention, "It is the lot of man", epitomises the poet. Thomson, Spenser and Milton hover behind the lines, as does Gray:

> And in this wilderness gay roses bloom
> Scenting the desart air with rich perfume

In one of the many versions in the Commonplace Book the poet uses that popular Gothic device, closely linked with the figure of the Wandering Jew, of the entrance of an 'aged man', who is both sage and outcast. The Ancient Mariner is the supreme example of this figure, while Charles Tennyson d'Eyncourt's effort in *Eustace* ends in banality, when the intruder is revealed as the disguised Eustace himself. At the heart of George's poem is the very characteristic contrast between the Fortunate and the Unfortunate Man and the note of querulousness is equally characteristic. The poet observes that 'It is a mingled destiny we share / E'en from the puling cradle to the tomb'. However, he contrasts those 'to whom in mercy or in ire / High heaven hath bid woe's chalice overflow' with those who 'barely skim the cup of sorrow / And gay through life's enamelled path advance', prefiguring, with gloomy delight, the downfall of such men. Charles was beloved of his parents, was noted for his success with women, was set on a career in the Law, was married to an heiress. He must indeed have seemed to his brother one of those

> Whose jocund hearts forgetful of tomorrow
> The festive bowl, the song, the wreathed dance
> And lovely woman's witching smiles entrance.

Trapped in Lincolnshire and struggling for financial security, George painfully captures his own state of mind as one who undergoes:

> All the variety of ills below
> That spring from poverty, contempt and pain
> Remorse with scorpions bound upon her brow
> And jealousy with murder in her train
> And baleful envy pining at another's gain

The personifications (akin to those in Keats's "Ode to Melancholy", published in 1817: George shared Keats's debt to Milton and Spenser) are powerful. Significantly the poet lists 'contempt' as second only to poverty in his share of ills. As his letters show it was his father's *contempt* which he found hardest to bear ("*Now you great awkward booby are you here*"). He leaps from this to 'Remorse... jealousy... murder... and baleful envy'. Here is the father in *Maud* before he was driven to suicide. The 'unadopted' last line ('And madness harassing the mind with fancies vain') suggests a threat to the writer's own sanity. It is as if he cannot make his life - or his verse - coherent because of the corroding effect of these negative emotions.

George's "Song" ("Mad Tom") deserves special attention. It is written in a bold and flowing hand with few cancellations, suggesting the confidence released in the poet by his adopting the guise of the Fool. There is extant a version of the poem in Alfred's hand - evidence of its significance for him, as a poet interested in manifestations of madness and evidence, too, perhaps that he had committed his father's work to memory. Certainly the poem has great psychological, if not literary, interest. The persona of 'Mad Tom' and the safety of the Bedlam Ballad form enable George to indulge the manic as opposed to the depressive side of his nature. The resonances from *King Lear*, in which the good son Edgar, disguised as Mad Tom, works to help his father, while the bastard son Edmund plots his downfall, could not have escaped George, so desperate for the role of 'good son' himself. This is also the closest approximation in his surviving work to a love poem to his wife, Eliza,[1] couched though his feelings are in references to disinheritance and madness:

---

1   George's line 'Oh then I'll breed a riot' also furnishes an appropriate collective noun for the Somersby Tennysons!

> I have no dirty acres
> To settle on my love
> But the flaming fields of space are mine
> And the canopy above.
>
> With heaven's studded concave
> I'll bind her forehead fair
> Her eyes shall be the Northern Lights
> And a comet's tail her hair.

The planets seem to have psychological significance. The mountains and even the sun and moon, symbols of male and female, are put in their place by 'Mad Tom', lunatic victim turned into all-powerful ruler:

> I'll climb those lofty mountains
> And there I'll fight the gypsies
> I'll play at bowls with the sun & moon
> And kick them to eclipses.

For once George's energy and exuberance enable him to overcome the oppression of his upbringing. Though he recognises his emotional poverty and still feels that he was born under Saturn, he here makes a bid for freedom and happiness:

> What tho' I'm poor I'll marry
> And then poor Tom will sing
> For Saturn rolls by my command
> And I'll marry with his ring.

———

George's direct influence on Alfred's poetic development during the years of tutoring at Somersby is undoubted but hard to assess.[1] When the boy produced an epic at the age of thirteen his father is recorded as saying that he 'would yet be one of the great in English Literature'.[2] Charles however insisted in later life that 'We had the greatest reverence for his learning, but my father never let us know what he thought of our poetry, used to tell us to mind our books, for that we could never get bread by such stuff....'[3] Certainly it was his father who encouraged Alfred, while at Cambridge, to enter for the Chancellor's Gold Medal (which he won with the poem "Timbuctoo") and it is just possible that he may have been behind the printing, in 1827, by Jacksons of Louth, of *Poems by Two Brothers*. These poems share with his a

[1]  Compare for example the comment made in a letter of 8 May 1866 by the (then retired) Headmaster of Louth School, the Revd John Waite, to Alfred: 'Some sixty years ago I have laughed and disputed, disputed and laughed, with your talented father, who was never so happy as when engaged in logomachy, and whose good temper would never admit of acerbity - but I was never more surprised when he undertook the completion of your education - for I remember that he used to lament that at school he had not been trained to versification, and classic elegance - which defects he must have wonderfully overcome; or perhaps the Etonian [Frederick] may have given his fraternal aid and talents....' (Beinecke Library, Yale).

[2]  Paden, p.117, note 34.

[3]  H. D. Rawnsley, *Memories of the Tennysons* (Glasgow, 1900), pp.50-51.

severe metrical correctness and a stylised treatment of emotions. Alfred's work in his early teens (a translation of Claudian's *Rape of Proserpine*[1] and "The Devil and the Lady") had shown much greater freedom and boldness.

*Poems by Two Brothers* is predictably adolescent in its preoccupation with the past and with death. Charles's contributions[2] include the revealing poem, "In early youth I lost my sire", in which he describes the giddiness of a young man deprived of his father, 'That fost'ring guide, which all require'. He is much simpler and more direct than Alfred. He writes straightforwardly "On the Death of My Grandmother", whereas Alfred's elegy (commissioned by his grandfather) is more impersonal - "And ask ye why these sad tears stream".[3]

Alfred's poems are grander than his brother's and more obviously ambitious. There is a great deal of exoticism (which Paden was the first to link with Alfred's reading in his father's library).[4] "Lamentation of the Peruvians", "The Expedition of Nadir Shah into Hindostan", "The Fall of Jerusalem", "Exhortation to the Greeks", and "Babylon" all suggest the range of the adolescent's interests; they are predominantly in dactylic tetrameters and the influence of Byron is evident:

> Bow, daughter of Babylon, bow thee to dust!
> Thine heart shall be quell'd, and thy pride shall be crush'd:
> Weep, Babylon, weep! for thy splendour is past;
> And they come like a storm in the day of the blast.

Much of the travelling, as with his father, is actually an inner journey, a restless fleeing from self. In George's 'O'er frozen seas', one of the discarded fragments from "The Wandering Jew" sequence, there is a Miltonic attempt to escape guilt and darkness:

> ... my restless flight
> The fiend impelled, from where for ever fast
> In chrystal chains pale Saturn lies and night
> Eternal reigns....

In "I wander in darkness and sorrow" and "Unhappy man, why wander there",[5] Alfred uses the same image of the restless exiled soul:

[1]   Paul Turner, *Tennyson* (London, 1976), p.35, observes: 'It describes something closely resembling Somersby Rectory at its worst: a Hell dominated by a gloomy tyrant, Pluto, bitterly resentful of his unjustly privileged brother, Jove. The translation stops just before the text of an angry message to the god of heaven, containing a complaint that might almost have been addressed by Dr Tennyson to his brother Charles at Bayons Manor: "Cruel brother, is it not enough that I should have to endure this hideous darkness, while you enjoy the light of the stars?"'

[2]   Identification of the brothers' contributions is given in the 1893 edition of *Poems by Two Brothers*. This includes a number of poems which had been omitted 'for some forgotten reason' from the edition of 1827.

[3]   A number of commentators, e.g. Martin, p.44, believe that Alfred's elegy to his grandmother has never been found - but this poem, printed immediately after Charles's direct tribute, must surely be it; see also *Poems A.T.*, I, p.127.

[4]   Paden, *passim*; also the annotations to the poems of 1827 in *Poems A.T.*, I.

[5]   Printed only in 1893; *Poems A.T.*, I, pp.167-68.

Whether in Afric's scorching clime,
  Or Lapland's wilds I flee,
I heed not season, place or time,
  They're all the same to me.

Ossian is also evident in the background of the poems ("Oh! ye wild winds" and "The Vale of Bones") and there is a sprinkling of conventional Christianity - "Why should we weep for those who die?" and "The Dying Man to His Friend"[1] - and one strangely prophetic poem, employing his father's favourite Spenserian stanzas, "Friendship":

O thou most holy Friendship! wheresoe'er
  Thy dwelling be....

The Thought of thine existence is so bright
With beautiful imaginings - the glance
  Upon thy fancied being such delight,
That I will deem thee Truth, so lovely is thy might!

The source of the idea has again been traced to a work in the Rectory library, J. Bigland's *Essays on Various Subjects*, 2 vols. (Doncaster, 1805);[2] it was to be made reality only a few years later in the meeting with Hallam.

There is a definite preoccupation with old age and with isolation. Paden suggests that this is a predictable adolescent displacement and declares that, in "The Old Sword" and "The Old Chieftain", 'the mask of age is... a device allowing comfortable compromise between fantasies of desired experience and realities of inexperience'.[3] However, running through these poems about old age, less predictably, is a strain of discontent, of lack of fulfilment, which suggests poignantly the extent of Alfred's identification with his father. George was only fifty-three when he died, but his powers had been in decline for some years, as Alfred's had been developing. It is difficult to imagine the emotions evident in "On a Dead Enemy", "Remorse", "The Grave of a Suicide" and "The Passions" as not in some way influenced by the cluster of contradictory feelings surrounding the paradoxical figure of Dr Tennyson - father, tutor, priest, scholar, spiritual guide, but also sinner, victim, worldly failure, source of life, whose own hold on life and sanity was so precarious. The Suicide figure is an obvious antecedent of the father in *Maud*; his misery and hysteria - and the sorrow he causes the woman who loves him - must all have been evident to the boy watching his mother's sufferings at the hand of the husband from whom, in 1829, she was forced to flee. The whole of "The Grave of a Suicide" smacks strongly of George's own central preoccupation in "It is the lot of man":

Poor soul! the dawning of thy life was dim;
  Frown'd the dark clouds upon thy natal day;

1   Printed only in 1893; *Poems A.T.*, I, p.166.
2   *Poems A.T.*, I, pp.125-26.
3   Paden, pp.60-61, 74.

Soon rose thy cup of sorrow to the brim,
    And hope itself but shed a doubtful ray.

That hope had fled, and all within was gloom;
    That hope had fled — thy woe to phrenzy grew;
For thou, wed to misery from the womb —
    Scarce one bright scene thy night of darkness knew!

"Oh! softly tread: in death he slumbers here;
    "'Tis here," she cries, "within his narrow cell!" —
The bitter sob, the wildly-starting tear,
    The quivering lip, proclaim the rest too well!

Alfred's verse contains no criticism of this woeful character. Pity is the over-riding emotion. The situation is seen as the result of misfortune rather than of personal inadequacy or ill-doing — and the same is true of the presentation of the father in *Maud*, a much more famous evocation of Dr Tennyson. In "Remorse" Alfred produces a powerful evocation of the outcast figure, strongly reminiscent of his father's "The Wandering Jew":

And I was cursed from my birth,
A reptile made to creep on earth,
An hopeless outcast, born to die
A living death eternally!

It is the figure of the hapless victim which so moves the young Alfred and this was certainly the role in which Dr Tennyson saw himself. Children are inevitably victims of their parents' self-dramatisations. The only literary evidence of latent aggression against a father so signally failing to set an example of strength and courage comes in Alfred's "On a Dead Enemy", where the boy finds an image which successfully combines hatred and pity in one sad form:

I came in haste with cursing breath,
    And heart of hardest steel;
But when I saw thee cold in death,
    I felt as man should feel.

For when I look upon that face,
    That cold, unheeding, frigid brow,
Where neither rage nor fear has place,
    By Heaven! I cannot hate thee now!

Perhaps the metrical inhibitions set up in *Poems by Two Brothers* were emblems of emotional inhibitions too. In "The Passions", Alfred describes strong passion using his father's image of the scorpion - ('Remorse with scorpions bound upon her brow / And jealousy with murder in her train / And baleful envy pining at another's gain') - and turns it into a warning against the passions in general. It is as if the youthful writer is admonishing himself to avoid the fate of his father:

Beware, beware, ere thou takest
    The draught of misery!

Beware, beware ere thou wakest
   The scorpions that sleep in thee!
...
... the slightest touch will waken
   Those pangs that will always grieve thee,
And thy soul will be fiercely shaken
   With storms that will never leave thee!

------

The power of Alfred's complex emotion about his father and his ruined life is evident long after *Poems by Two Brothers*, and infuses much of his greatest as well as his weakest work. It is there in the aimless wandering of "Ulysses" (written October 1833; published 1842); it is there, too, in "Tithon" (written 1833; revised for publication as "Tithonus" in 1859). The 'sentence of eternal life', for example, which Dr Tennyson gave his Wandering Jew is that which Alfred gives to Tithon/Tithonus. George simply points a moral, with cautious metrical accuracy:

   ...
   O yet at last revoke thy fearful doom
   Let mercy temper judgment, let thy sword
   Of vengeance slumber, and the silent tomb
   My ever tortur'd heart and wearied limbs enwomb.

   How vain the prayer! I bear a charmed life,
   I tarry till he comes; such is the decree
   Of him who sav'd the world, and neither knife
   Rope, rack, nor pois'nous herb, nor malady
   Fire, earth, nor air can ever set me free....

The first line anticipates Tithon's anguished cry, 'Ah! keep me not for ever in the East' (revised as 'Yet hold me not forever in thine East' when Alfred reworked the material in "Tithonus") - yet the contrast with "Tithon" (and "Tithonus") reveals instructively the huge gulf between the two men as poets. Alfred is not concerned to point a moral; instead he evokes sensuously the struggle of love and life against the coldness of death.

     The echo of George's poetic voice is clearest, unexpectedly, in the great lyric poems. George's "The Minstrel's Lament" anticipates the languor and sensuous nostalgia of the "The Lotos-Eaters" (1832; revised 1842), written, in part, in his father's favourite Spenserian stanza. George uses an elegiac quatrain:

   Sweet is their memory as the dying close
   Of musick heard afar; soft as the breeze
   Which faintly whispers thro' the slumb'ring trees
   In twilight's calm repose.

   Sweet as the bells upon the varying gale
   When mellowed by the wave; soft as the tear
   Which melts in beauty's eye, at sorrow's prayer
   And flows at pity's tale.

> Sweet as the perfume of the fading rose;
> Soft as the moon reflected from the deep
> In eve autumnal when the waters sleep
> And not a zephyr blows.

In the 'Choric Song' from "The Lotos-Eaters" a similar languor is conveyed in more daring metrical flights:

> There is sweet music here that softer falls,
> Than petals from blown roses on the grass,
> Or nightdews on still waters between walls
> Of shadowy granite, in a gleaming pass.
> Music that gentlier on the spirit lies,
> Than tir'd eyelids upon tir'd eyes....
> ...
> How sweet it were, hearing the downward stream,
> With halfshut eyes ever to seem
> Falling asleep in a halfdream!

There is much to remind one too of 'Now sleeps the crimson petal, now the white' (perhaps Alfred's most sensuous lyric) and even more of 'Tears, idle tears' written in 1834 (both are embedded in *The Princess*).[1] There is the same strange mixture of emotions - 'sweet yet mournful' - and Tennyson must surely have *heard* the rhythms and vowel sounds of his father's 'sweet... soft' antithesis as he wrote:

> Fresh as the first beam glittering on a sail,
> That brings our friends up from the underworld,
> Sad as the last which reddens over one
> That sinks with all we love below the verge;
> So sad, so fresh, the days that are no more

Tennyson seems most responsive to his father's voice, then, when in lyrical mood. Certainly too he owes to his father his earliest sense of the Poet as Outsider, threatened by an unsympathetic world and tempted to build a Palace of Art ; but most of all he seems to absorb from the troubled doctor a pervasive wistfulness in which hope is made by an act of will to triumph over despair, although it is often despair which leaves the stronger impression.

———

In only four poems, three from *Poems, Chiefly Lyrical* (London, 1830) and one from *Poems* (London, 1832/3), does Tennyson refer directly to his parents. In "Isabel" (1830) there is a tribute to his mother (whose sweet nature and religious disposition so strongly suggest her own mother-in-law, Mary Tennyson, and her future

---

1    'Tears, idle tears' was written according to Tennyson in the autumn of 1834 when he visited Tintern Abbey, 'full for me of its bygone memories. It is the sense of the abiding in the transient.' Only a short distance away was Clevedon, where Hallam was buried (*Poems A.T.*, II, p.232; Martin, pp.193-94); Dr Tennyson, however, must surely have been present in Alfred's memories. Another work where Tennyson's grief for Hallam blurs into grief for his father is "Morte d'Arthur" (written 1833/4; published 1842), which Paden, pp.86-87 sees as strongly connected with the notion of Dr Tennyson as the Great Father.

daughter-in-law, Emily Sellwood). Here the loving son finds an image for his parents' marriage as it appeared to his closely-observing eyes, and in doing so gives the lie to those biographers who dismiss Eliza as ineffectual. She could, he implies, recognise her husband's weakness for what it was, since she possessed

> The intuitive decision of a bright
> And thoroughedgéd intellect to part
> Error from crime....

He praises, as twentieth-century commentators are less inclined to do, her ability to endure, to uphold her marriage vows, not to rebel. She had, as she herself was to say to her father-in-law,

> The laws of wifehood charactered in gold
> Upon the blenchéd tablets of her heart.

Most tellingly, Alfred displays a mature understanding of the way in which the marriage survived, as a relationship based on emotional need on one side and the need to give on the other. Eliza's goodness, if it had not been drawn upon by her demanding husband, he implies, would have gone to waste:

> A leaning and upbearing parasite,
> Clothing the stem, which else had fallen quite,
> With clustered flowerbells and ambrosial orbs
> Of rich fruitbunches leaning on each other -
> Shadow forth thee: - the world hath not another
> (Though all her fairest forms are types of thee,
> And thou of God in thy great charity),
> Of such a finished chastened purity.

The "Ode to Memory" (1830) makes a brief topographical reference to the Rectory - 'The seven elms, the poplars four / That stand beside my father's door...'. In "Song [A spirit haunts the year's last hours]" (1830) there is no direct autobiographical reference, but Tennyson presents an image of morbidity and melancholy which powerfully suggests the brooding presence ruling the Rectory. This presence is linked to the Old Year - in other words, it must be left behind if the future is to be embraced. Decayed promise is suggested in the rose, hollyhock, tiger-lily, anticipating the garden in *Maud* (where a bereaved son is wooed back to life by love).[1] This poem is a complex and successful evocation of filial emotion, including an anticipation of the death of the father and the sense of 'something rotten' which is nevertheless peculiarly attractive:

> A SPIRIT haunts the year's last hours
> Dwelling amid these yellowing bowers:
> To himself he talks;
> For at eventide, listening earnestly,
> At his work you may hear him sob and sigh
> In the walks;

---

1    Cf the description of the Rectory garden in his "Ode to Memory": '... bowered close / with pleachéd alleys of the trailing rose, / Long alleys falling down to twilight grots, / Or opening upon level plots / Of crownéd lilies, standing near / Purple-spikéd lavender....'

Earthward he boweth the heavy stalks
Of the mouldering flowers:
　　Heavily hangs the broad sunflower
　　　Over its grave i' the earth so chilly;
　　Heavily hangs the hollyhock,
　　　Heavily hangs the tigerlily.

The air is damp, and hushed, and close
As a sick man's room when he taketh repose
　　　An hour before death;
My very heart faints and my whole soul grieves
At the moist rich smell of the rotting leaves,
　　　And the breath
　　Of the fading edges of box beneath,
And the year's last rose.
　　Heavily hangs the broad sunflower
　　　Over its grave i' the earth so chilly;
　　Heavily hangs the hollyhock,
　　　Heavily hangs the tigerlily.

In the 1832 volume Tennyson, immediately after his father's death in March 1831, returns to the uncomplicated tone of *Poems by Two Brothers*, that of simple piety. In "To J.S." he is sympathising with his friend, James Spedding, on the loss of his brother:

'Tis strange that those we lean on most,
　　Those in whose laps our limbs are nurst,
Fall into shadow, soonest lost:
　　Those we love first are taken first.

God gives us love. Something to love
　　He lends us; but when love is grown
To ripeness, that on which it throve
　　Falls off, and love is left alone.

This is the curse of time. Alas!
　　In grief I am not all unlearned:
Once thro' mine own doors Death did pass;
　　One went, who never hath returned.

He will not smile - not speak to me
　　Once more. Two years his chair is seen
Empty before us. That was he
　　Without whose life I had not been.

The language, particularly of the first stanza quoted, suggests the death of a mother rather than a father, while the entwining imagery of the following stanza is reminiscent of "Isabel". In both poems there seems almost a fusion of the parent figures into a single image of security. What the young poet saw in his home may not have been happiness, but it was certainly a genuine marriage.

# INFLUENCE ON ALFRED TENNYSON

The stanza form of "To J.S." was praised by Hallam (Ricks suggests that this may have led Tennyson into developing it after his friend's death into the *In Memoriam* stanza).[1] The grief expressed in the later poem surely involves grief rekindled for the death of a father - a grief which is both painful and liberating. In Section CIII of *In Memoriam* Tennyson describes the departure from Somersby (which took place in 1835), seeing it essentially as the abandoning of his father's grave. Once again he refers to a 'leaning and upbearing parasite', the woodbine:

> Our father's dust is left alone
> And silent under other snows:
> There in due time the woodbine blows,
> The violet comes, but we are gone.

The next lyric is the triumphant, life-embracing 'Ring out, wild bells'. Diana Basham argues persuasively that this specifically refers to Tennyson's jubilant release into a new maturity from his father's dark shadow.[2] We would add that this movement has been prefigured both in the 1830 volume, in "A spirit haunts the year's last hours" and in the poem which precedes "To J.S." in the 1832 volume, "The Death of the Old Year". The notion of starting afresh, of beginning a new stage in life, is thus linked several times with the casting off of Dr Tennyson. In "The Death of the Old Year", written only months after his father's death, his son can vividly evoke a deathbed:

> And tho' his foes speak ill of him,
> He was a friend to me....
>    I've half a mind to die with you,
>    Old year, if you must die.
> ...
> To see him die, across the waste
> His son and heir doth ride posthaste,
> But he'll be dead before.
> ....
> How hard he breathes! Over the snow
> I heard just now the crowing cock.
> The shadows flicker to and fro:
> The cricket chirps: the light burns low:
> 'Tis nearly one o'clock.
> ...
> His face is growing sharp and thin.
> Alack! Our friend is gone.
> Close up his eyes: tie up his chin:
> Step from the corpse, and let him in
> That standeth there alone,
>    And waiteth at the door...

1   *Poems A.T.*, I, p.504.
2   Diana Basham, 'Tennyson and his fathers: the legacy of manhood in Tennyson's poems', *T.R.B.*, 4,4 (1985), pp.163-78.

The Tennysons were, despite their grumbling, a robustly healthy family. There had been no earlier family deaths at the Rectory in Alfred's lifetime: yet he deals here almost jauntily with a deathbed which was bound to recall that of his father so short a time before. Already, it seems, he is experiencing his father's departure from his life as a liberation.

————

The general sense of threat, of impending doom, which characterises much of Alfred's early poetry, re-emerges most powerfully in *Maud* (London, 1855). Here at last Alfred's imaginative closeness to his father receives triumphal artistic expression, a triumph built on fear of madness.[1]

In "The Flight" (written *c*.1836; published 1885) occurs the telling line, 'My father's madness makes me mad....', a line which might well sum up the biographical genesis of *Maud*. At the end of *Maud* the hero finds an acceptable outlet for his aggression and a cure for his misery in War; there is a sense of relief at the escape from the dangers of the frighteningly personal. The father's suicide before the poem begins (linked to envy of a rival, a former friend, whose family inhabit the beautiful Hall as brother Charles's family inhabited Bayons) suggests the terror his own father's mental state must have caused the poet years before. George's violence, turned in the 1820s against his wife and children, seemed (to outsiders as well as to his family) to be liable to be turned upon himself. Alfred's fear for his father's life must have been linked to fear *of* his father; yet tenderness seems to have suppressed in Alfred and young Charles the (more normal?) aggression evinced by Frederick. It is important for an understanding of Alfred's development as a poet as well as as a man to realise that normal oedipal rivalry was in him neutered by protectiveness towards a suffering victim. (It is perhaps instructive to compare this with Dickens's feeling for an equally inadequate father, and its effect on his art.) If emotion, even in the greatest poems, seems muted, forced towards consolation and away from pain (as at the end of *In Memoriam*), then this early inhibition should be remembered. In the 1862 edition of the *Idylls of the King*, Tennyson included his 'Dedication' in memory of the Prince Consort who had died in December 1861. Tennyson praised the way Albert, an ideal father with an ideal family, had lived:

> With what sublime repression of himself,
> And in what limits, and how tenderly....

Here Tennyson is both quintessentially Victorian and very much the product of his own family's tensions.

Alfred composed *Maud* after his move to Farringford, Isle of Wight, in November 1853. The germ of the poem was the lyric "Oh! that 'twere possible", written soon after Hallam's death in 1833/4, and published in *The Tribute* (London,

[1]  Cf. Michel Foucault's *Madness and Civilisation*, 'The moment when, together, the work of art and madness are born and fulfilled is the beginning of the time when the world finds itself arraigned by that work of art and responsible before it for what it is.' We are indebted to Roger S. Platizsky, *A Blueprint of His Dissent. Madness and Method in Tennyson's Poetry* (Lewisburg, London and Toronto, 1989), p.11 for this reference.

1837). In the same collection was an anonymous ballad with a medieval setting, "The
Wicked Nephew":

> Then slowly spake that ancient man,
>     For the shade of the tomb was on his brow,
> "Castle and lands are thine, Nephew,
>     "For thou hast slain thine Uncle now.
>
> "Castle and lands are thine, Nephew,
>     "So high the hall, so broad the lea,
> "When I am but a seely ghost
>     "There's room enow for thee and me.
>
> "Face to face i'the hall we'll sit,
>     "Side by side we'll tread the lea,
> "And aye by day and aye by night
>     "My sprite shall bear thee company."
>
> Then down he sank, that aged man,
>     And breath'd his last on the good green sward;
> Nor yet a word his Nephew spake,
>     But wiped his life-blood from his sword.

Alfred did not have a copy of his poem with him and had to send for one from his
father-in-law; however, it seems more than likely that he had read the ballad (with its
echoes of *Hamlet* and a character called Maud)[1] and in a strange way the poem he
eventually produced, with its fantasia on family themes and its fierce attack on the
hated figure of his Uncle Charles, enemy and yet also doppelganger, must have
seemed to him the work of a 'wicked nephew'. Alfred was later to refer to the poem
as his 'little Hamlet'.[2] What he meant by this, presumably, was simply that in it a
son seeks to avenge a father's death. As Ernest Jones suggests in *Hamlet and Oedipus*
(London, 1947), his famous essay on the play, the theatrical Hamlet is hindered in
this aim by a secret and unacknowledged identification with the murderer, the hated
uncle. Charles Tennyson d'Eyncourt loomed behind the poem, as he loomed in
Alfred's imagination. It is indeed in its genesis a Poem of Two Brothers.

Ralph Wilson Rader's *Tennyson's Maud: The Biographical Genesis* (Berkeley and
Los Angeles, 1963) has convincingly adumbrated the biographical background of the
poem. More recently Susan Shatto has suggested that Farringford was not only
Alfred's first permanent home since leaving Somersby, but was also, with its
'gothicized Georgian architecture', a tangible reminder of the Rectory, which sent
his thoughts back to the early days.[3] Rader's aim, in Shatto's words, was 'to propose

---

1    See George O. Marshall, Jr., 'Giftbooks, Tennyson, and *The Tribute* (1837)', *The Georgia
     Review* XVI, 4 (Winter, 1962), pp.459-64.
2    See, for example, Betty Miller, 'Tennyson: the early years', *The Twentieth Century*, 167
     (June, 1960), pp.520-29, who picks up this reference and goes on to make an interesting
     comparison with the story of Geraint in the *Idylls of the King* in which the situation is
     reversed (p.525).
3    Susan Shatto (ed.), *Tennyson's Maud. A Definitive Edition* (London, 1986), p.2.

associations between specific events and relationships of Tennyson's youth and the poem of his maturity'.[1] Our aim here is slightly different: it is to suggest that the power of the poem comes, not only from a general recollection of family tensions, but from a direct identification of the poet with his father, and a suppressed identification with his uncle, from which emerges the sense of a self divided; it is thus self division which gives the work its power.

The poem begins, like *Hamlet*, with a reference to the past, to the death of the father as the result of betrayal. Behind that betrayal looms a demonic figure based (however unfairly) on that bogeyman of the Somersby Tennysons, 'The Old Man of the Wolds':

> But that old man, now lord of the broad estate and the Hall
> Dropt off gorged from a scheme that had left us flaccid and drain'd.

The struggle depicted in *Maud* is therefore a peculiarly personal one. Personal too, and of great oedipal power, is the presentation of the mother's love:

> Would there be sorrow for *me*? There was *love* in the passionate shriek,
> Love for the silent thing that had made false haste to the grave -
> Wrapt in a cloak, as I saw him, and thought he would rise and speak
> And rave at the lie and the liar, ah God, as he used to rave.

This is the imaginative landscape of "A spirit haunts the year's last hours" and of "Isabel". One recalls Elizabeth Tennyson's loving tribute to the husband who had made her life a misery and Alfred's words to the clergyman who officiated at her funeral: 'indeed she was the beautifulest thing God Almighty ever did make'.[2] In this light the verses dealing with the narrator's youth have an especial poignancy:

> ... my dark-dawning youth,
> Darken'd watching a mother decline
> And that dead man at her heart and mine:
> For who was left to watch her but I?
> Yet so did I let my freshness die.

> ... I felt she was slowly dying,
> Vext with lawyers and harass'd with debt:
> For how often I caught her with eyes all wet,
> Shaking her head at her son and sighing
> A world of trouble within!

Just as the poem's troubled narrator takes upon himself the burdens of his father, so Tennyson himself absorbs his father's enmities and creates a situation very like the one the Somersby Tennysons had imagined to be the truth. It is a simplified and exaggerated account of the complex personalities involved and all the more powerful for that.

> When have I bow'd to her father, the wrinkled head of the race?
> I met her to-day with her brother, but not to her brother I bow'd....

---

[1]    *ibid.*, p.37.
[2]    Tennyson & Dyson, p.95.

The descriptions of the brother are surely more extensive than the role demands and suggest the depth of Alfred's feelings about Uncle Charles. In the 1820s and 1830s, Charles's success in politics paralleled George's decline. Besides, his political development shocked the rest of the family, including, one suspects, his more cautiously conservative nephew. Though his instincts in poetry were conservative, Charles poured his political energies into the Liberal cause. In 1820 he took up the cause of Queen Caroline against the king; in 1826 he brought about the banning of man-traps and spring-guns; and in 1832, while Alfred in Cambridge stood with other students against the labourers rioting for more rights, Charles in London worked unstintingly for the cause of Reform. It was incomprehensible to the self-absorbed, non-political Somersby Tennysons that their uncle, already crippled by sciatica in London, should put before his brother's funeral attendance in the House for the crucial Reform Bill vote.

In *Maud* Alfred allows his accumulated dislike full rein. He attacks his uncle, as his own, not his father's, rival. The emotional identification with his father is complete. He attacks a 'gewgaw castle... / New as his title, built last year' which recalls Charles's Bayons Manor (though the context also suggests Brancepeth, again his uncle's handiwork) 'pricking a cockney ear' across the moor. Most vehemently he attacks Bulwer-Lytton - and here the interlocking of his own and his uncle's life is strongest.

Bulwer-Lytton had already famously attacked Tennyson's 1832 volume in the *New Monthly Magazine* of January 1833 for its 'effeminacies' and 'eunuch strain', and in *The New Timon* (London, 1846): 'Let School-Miss Alfred vent her chaste delight / On "darling little rooms so warm and bright!"' Six years older than Alfred, he was Charles's closest friend and supporter. Alfred regained the initiative in his bitter assault on Bulwer in "The New Timon, and the Poets" (*Punch*, 28 February 1846) where the (earlier) charge of effeminacy is unforgettably returned: 'The padded man - that wears the stays- // Who kill'd the girls and thrill'd the boys / With dandy pathos... / A dapper boot - a little hand....'[1] The effect of sexual rivalry is compounded when one recalls that Alfred was particularly fond of his cousin Julia - he wrote at least one poem with her as Muse - and that Julia's retreat to a convent (later in 1846) was prompted - though Alfred could not have known this - by her thwarted passion for Bulwer-Lytton.

What Alfred loathes in both Charles and Bulwer is what he sees as an insincere and self-indulgent dandyism:

... that dandy-despot, he,
That jewell'd mass of millinery,
That oil'd and curl'd Assyrian Bull

1    Late in life, Alfred wrote a short account of the background to his attack on Bulwer-Lytton which makes it clear he had not forgotten the differences between the Somersby and Tealby branches: 'Moreover [Bulwer] stated in a note that I belonged to a very rich family — the younger son, his friend [Tennyson d'Eyncourt], who had inherited, was rich enough, but the other branch was shut out in the cold & at that time I had scarce anything' (T.R.C. N5).

> Smelling of musk and of insolence,
> Her brother...

The account of the father, 'A gray old wolf and a lean', who lives elsewhere, certainly fits 'The Old Man of the Wolds'. What matters of course is not exact equivalences but the evidence that Tennyson chose to inhabit his father's imagination, to recreate at such a distance in time *his* enmities, to vent *his* spleen on those long dead:

> Not that old gray wolf, for he came not back
> From the wilderness, full of wolves, where he used to lie;
> He has gather'd the bones for his o'ergrown whelp to crack;
> Crack them now for yourself, and howl, and die.

There is even a duel, recalling Uncle Charles's escapade in 1831. Echoes of Dr Tennyson's wide-ranging bitterness are there too in the diatribe against the narrator's rival whose grandfather made money from coal, and is now

> Gone to a blacker pit, for whom
> Grimy nakedness dragging his trucks
> And laying his trams in a poison'd gloom
> Wrought, till he crept from a gutted mine
> Master of half a servile shire....

Elizabeth Russell certainly saw this as an attack on her late husband. Though Tennyson denied the charge[1] (again, exact equivalences are not the real issue) he seems to have accurately captured the bitterness his father felt towards all those whom he classified as having worldly advantage over him.

Most accurate of all is the depiction of a mind struggling with madness and swinging from the manic to the murderous: such acute analysis is surely based on long years of close observation:

> So dark a mind within me dwells,
>     And I make myself such evil cheer,
> That if I be dear to someone else,
>     Then someone else may have much to fear....

> So now I have sworn to bury
> All this dead body of hate,
> I feel so free and so clear
> By the loss of that dead weight,
> That I should grow light-headed, I fear,
> Fantastically merry....

What is significant here is Tennyson's ability to convey fear *for* and fear *of* the figure of the narrator. He is simultaneously his father and the victim of his father. He captures in fact the exact emotional position of the maturing adolescent who must kill the father in order to come into his own. To do so, he must adopt and come to terms with his father's enemies. Hence the successful uncle in life becomes the successful rival in the poem - and here the psychological links with *Hamlet* are

---

[1]    *Memoir*, I, pp.407-08; *Letters A.T.*, II, p.155.

peculiarly powerful. Hamlet, according to Ernest Jones, cannot kill his uncle, much as he wishes to do so, because ultimately he identifies with him. Like Uncle Charles, Alfred unwittingly threatened his father with his own success: the powerful son is always and inevitably his father's rival as well as his successor. Alfred and Uncle Charles both desire success and as it were steal it from George, just as Claudius and Hamlet both desire Gertrude. In Ernest Jones's words, 'Hamlet's moral fate is bound up with his uncle's for good or ill. In reality his uncle incorporates the deepest and most buried part of his own personality....'[1] Hamlet's solution in the play is to bring about his own death; the narrator's answer in *Maud* is to transfer his hatred to his country's enemy. War is the acceptable public face of private passion. Alfred's own solution was, towards the end of his life, to take on the trappings of his uncle's life, to embrace public success and leave behind the father he had loved and pitied.

The beginning was made in the years following his Uncle Charles's death, when, according to family tradition, his daughter Clara reconciled the two branches of the family. Alfred was closer to his uncle in temperament and interests than he ever acknowledged directly. Their lives in retrospect seem strangely counterpointed. Both worked assiduously at their chosen careers. Both held naively and stubbornly to a vision of medieval innocence. Both had a streak of old-maidish timidity and respectability beneath dashingly handsome exteriors. Both were blest with a loyal eldest son; each lost a younger son in tragic circumstances and tried to make reparation in verse.[2] In later years Alfred followed his uncle's example, retreating into his own Palace of Art, Aldworth, designed by James Knowles (from the Tennysons' sketches and plans) and built at great expense between 1868 and 1870.[3] Tennyson's architectural imagination turned out to be as simple as his uncle's poetic imagination in *Eustace*. Similarly his successes and failures in the *Idylls of the King* (which he was amending into the final week of his life) parallel Charles's at Bayons. Both attempt to understand and reinterpret their age in 'Operatic Gothic' - at once grand and absurd. In 1876 Tennyson dedicated his play *Harold* to Bulwer-Lytton's son, the second Baron Lytton, in words which reveal the poet's deep though reluctant recognition of kinship with his uncle: 'Your father dedicated his "Harold" to my father's brother; allow me to dedicate my "Harold" to yourself.' In 1883, when he was offered a peerage, Tennyson first considered the titles Lord d'Eyncourt

---

1    Ernest Jones, *Hamlet and Oedipus* (London, 1947), p.88.

2    Tennyson's son Lionel (born 1854) died returning from India in April 1886. Tennyson's "Locksley Hall Sixty Years After" (1886) alludes to the event; Lionel's death is the subject of "To the Marquis of Dufferin and Ava" (1889).

3    See especially Priscilla Metcalf, *James Knowles, Victorian Editor and Architect* (Oxford, 1980), pp.197-208; also Martin, pp.472-76. Alfred had visited Bayons on at least two occasions. Mrs Fanny Tennyson d'Eyncourt wrote to George Hildeyard from Usselby on 29 June 1837: 'Julia & I have called at Caistor where we saw Mrs. Turner.... They since have been to see the house at Tealby & had tea there along with Alfred....' (L.A.O. T.d'E. H121/52). On 25 July 1857, when staying with the Turners (at Grasby), Charles drove Alfred and Emily to Tealby: 'Only Mrs. d'Eyncourt at home. She is very kind & shows us all over the house', James O. Hoge (ed.), *Emily Tennyson's Journal* (Charlottesville, Virginia, 1981), p.96.

and Baron Tennyson d'Eyncourt[1] - the ultimate disloyalty to the memory of his father. In "Locksley Hall Sixty Years After" (1886) he was even able, albeit somewhat grudgingly, to forgive 'The Old Man of the Wolds':

> Gone the tyrant of my youth, and mute below the chancel stones,
> All his virtues - I forgive them - black in white above his bones.

Tennyson had broken free from the melancholic grip of that spirit which 'haunts the year's last hours' - but the cost in both artistic and personal terms was great. In turning his attention from the lyric to the dramatic he was moving from private vision to absorption in a public role.[2]

———

We hope to have shown that these Poems by Two Brothers have a resonance in Tennyson's life and work - that to understand his greatness one must understand what he shared with a father whom he loved and pitied and feared, perhaps in equal measure, and with an uncle whom he affected to despise, but whose name, whose fiction of their shared ancestry, he later in life aspired to take as his own. The voice of the loving yet pitying son and of the envious yet emulative nephew are there in Tennyson's greatest poetry. In his own way he cultivated his father's and uncle's minor talents and brought them to fruition in his work - in "Amphion" (written 1837/8; published 1842) he supplies the metaphor himself:

> My father left a park to me,
>   But it is wild and barren,
> A garden too with scarce a tree
>   And waster than a warren:
> Yet say the neighbours when they call,
>   It is not bad but good land,
> And in it is the germ of all
>   That grows within the woodland.[3]

1   Martin, p.543; also *Letters A.T.*, III, pp.271-72.
2   There are of course excellent lyrics from the later years, but the plays do suggest a mistaken sense of public vocation.
3   We owe this quotation to Diana Basham, 'Tennyson and his fathers', p.163. The date of composition is perhaps not without significance: the Tennysons left Somersby Rectory for High Beech, Epping in 1837.

# APPENDIX

### To My Dear Brother Eustace
by
Julia Tennyson d'Eyncourt[1]

I will not weep for thee
I will not weep for thee
For thy spirit is now
Far more happy and free
Than it could be below
        My Brother.

The gay rose thou did'st plant
Still climbs the sunny wall
'Tis the fairest to bloom
But the soonest to fall
Sweet emblem of thy doom
        My Brother.

The spring revives each flower
We for thy sake cherish
As sweet their scent they give
Tho' frail, they do not perish
But with thy mem'ry live
        My Brother.

The three trees thou did'st love
And Sisters thou did'st name
Lift their proud crests as high
As tho' now 'twere the same
As when thou still wert nigh
        My Brother.

Oft gaily would'st thou talk
Of all thy days to come
The trophies thou would'st bring
To deck thy Father's home
Bright hope thy thoughts did wing
        My Brother.

[1] H.R.O. D/EK C18/128. c.1842. The manuscript bears an endorsement by Bulwer-Lytton: 'By Julia D'Eyncourt 1st cousin to Alfred Tennyson: - She turned Roman Catholic & became a nun. She was beautiful & accomplished.'

Albeit thy spirit brave
All danger would have dared
When Glory, Honour, bade —
Thy gentle heart was spared,
No gore's on thy sheath'd blade
        My Brother.

The glad and cheering tone
Of thy sweet kindly voice
That sadness charm'd away
And all did so rejoice
Its echo hath left for aye
        My Brother.

Thy slender graceful form
Sometimes I think I see
Bound light up yonder hill
And hear thy shout of glee
At Eve, when all is still
        My Brother.

Thou livest in our hearts
Tho' thine responds no more
But the key-note of our mirth
That tone, none can restore
'Tis lost, 'tis past from earth
        My Brother.

I hear thy last farewell
I see thy tearful eye
Thy fondest smile was vain
Our tears to chase away
E'en now they spring again
        My Brother.

Then little we dreamt to hear
Thy knell boom o'er the wave
But since alas! thou'rt laid
So young in thy far grave
O'er Hope is cast a shade -
        My Brother.

## JULIA TENNYSON D'EYNCOURT

"Blest are the pure in heart"
So surely thou art blest
But may not those who love
Still hope to share thy rest
Thy home of love above?
    My Brother.


And to thy Mem'ry sounds
That bell thou can'st not hear
And ev'ry hour it tolls
Brings those to thee more near
No other hope consoles -
    My Brother.

# SELECT BIOGRAPHICAL INDEX

Hallam, Arthur, 40, 119n, 125, 128n, 132
Hallam, Henry, 40, 58n
Hamilton, Emma (née Russell), 32, 36, 47, 54n, 55n, 56
Harrison, Dr, 8, 9, 16, 28
Harrison, Henry, 18n, 42 & n, 43
Harrison, John, 18 & n, 42n (Figs 1 & 2)
Heneage, Mr, 1, 4
Heneage, George Robert, 14, 15, 20
Hildyard, Christopher, 44
Horlins (coachman at Somersby), 18, 29
Hutchinson, Mr, 2, 4
Hutton, Fanny, *see* Tennyson d'Eyncourt, Fanny
Hutton, Marianne, 58

Ingilby, Sir William, 26, 40

Jacksons of Louth (booksellers and printers), vii, 10, 12, 123
Jowett, Dr, 15

Knowles, James, 137

Langton, Bennet, 20n
Lackington (bookseller), 12
Lytton, E. R. Bulwer, 1st Earl of Lytton, 137

Macready, William, 52n
Marlhion family, 32
Melbourne, Lord, 44-45, 50
Mordaunt, Lieut Henry, 100n

Nicholson, W. A., 47, 48

Orme, Dr, 2

Paterson, John, 18n
Pennington, Mr, 34n
Pitt, Jane, 44
Potts (builder at Bayons Manor), 47
Pycock, George, 7

Rawnsley, T. H., 15n, 26-27, 31, 33-34, 36, 38
Russell, Elizabeth (née Tennyson), 1, 3-4, 7, 10, 22-26, 27, 31 & n, 32, 36 & n, 40, 43, 46, 50,
   53, 54, 55-56 & ns, 57, 71, 74, 91, 92, 93, 117-118, 120, 121, 136; *(frontispiece)*
Russell, Emma, *see* Hamilton, Emma
Russell, Matthew, 10, 18, 22, 47, 136.
Russell, William, 18n, 44-45, 50, 55-56

Salvin, Anthony, 42-43, 47
Scamblesby, Mrs, 14

Scarsdale, Earls of, 44
Sellwood, Emily, 129
Sellwood, Henry, 133
Sharpe (servant at Bayons Manor), 33
Simkiss, James, 53
Smith, H. Porter, 56
Spedding, James, 130
Stark (builder at Bayons Manor), 47

Tennyson, Alfred, vii-viii, 2, 8, 12, 20, 21, 27, 38, 39, 40, 54, 57, 58, 59
    Family influences: father, vii-viii, 119-20, 123-28, 129-32, 133-34 136-38; mother, 128-129;
        George Tennyson, vii, 124 & n, 134, 136, 138; Charles Tennyson d'Eyncourt, vii, 133,
        134-38; Julia Tennyson (d'Eyncourt), 92

    "Amphion", 138 & n
    "And ask ye why these sad tears stream", 124
    "Babylon", 124 & n
    "Charge of the Light Brigade, The", 58
    "Coach of Death, The", 88
    "Death of the Old Year, The", 131-32
    "Devil and the Lady, The", 124
    "Dying Man to His Friend, The", 125
    "Exhortation to the Greeks", 124
    "Expedition of Nadir Shah into Hindostan, The", 124
    "Fall of Jerusalem, The", 124
    "Flight, The", 132
    "Friendship", 125
    "Grave of a Suicide, The", 125-26
    *Harold*, 137
    "High Priest to Alexander, The", 82
    *Idylls of the King*, 132, 133n, 137
    "I wander in darkness and sorrow", 124
    *In Memoriam*, vii, 54, 57, 131, 132; 'Ring out wild bells', 131; 'Tonight ungathered let us
      leave', 131
    "Isabel", 128-29
    "Lamentation of the Peruvians", 124
    "Locksley Hall Sixty Years After", 137n, 138
    "Lotos-Eaters, The", 127-28
    "Mad Tom" [version of his father's poem], 88-89, 120, 122
    Maud, 58-59, 119, 122, 125, 129, 132-37
    "New Timon, and the Poets, The", 121, 135
    "Ode to Memory", 129 & n
    "Oh! that 'twere possible", 132, 133
    "Oh! ye wild winds", 125
    "Old Chieftan, The", 125
    "Old Sword, The", 125
    "On a Dead Enemy", 125, 126
    "Passions, The", 125, 126-27
    "Persia", 82

# LIST OF SUBSCRIBERS

B. G. Aldred, Peterborough.
Dr R. W. Ambler, Grimsby.
Susan Anstruther, London (two copies).
Rev. Raymond Ashling, Kettlestone, Norfolk.
Coun. the Rev. Bill Baker, Sutton on Sea.
Dr Diana Basham, Kenilworth.
Baylor University, Armstrong Browning Library, Waco, Texas.
D. L. Bird, Shoreham-by-Sea, West Sussex.
Sybil Blossom, Louth.
R. D. Borrill, Marshchapel, Grimsby.
Douglas Boyce, Market Rasen.
Alex Bridge, Felpham, Bognor Regis.
Mr and Mrs K. G. Brown, South Bretton, Peterborough.
Donald Campbell, Hornsey, London.
Cheyne Lane Bookshop, Stamford.
Dr Barbara Clark, Atlanta, Georgia.
Peter and Linda Clay, Peterborough.
Mrs Mavis Clynch, San Bernadino, California.
Patrick Cormack, House of Commons, London.
Charlotte Corser, York.
Claude Cox Books, Ipswich (three copies).
Ms Alison Crosland, London.
Mrs Jane Crowley, Brigsley, Grimsby (four copies).
Marion Cutforth, Easton-on-the-Hill, Stamford.
M. F. D'Alcorn, Wrentham, Beccles.
Peter Davy, London.
Dr and Mrs H. M. Drake, Louth.
R. Drury, Lincoln.
Roger Evans, the British Library, London.
S. E. Gilks, Peterborough.
Mrs J. M. Gooder, Newnham College, Cambridge (two copies).
Mrs E. E. D. Haigh, Barton, Cambridge.
Bryan Hall, Aylsham, Norfolk (two copies).
Dr Michael Hill, Kirkheaton, Huddersfield.
Richard Hollingsworth, Scunthorpe.
Mrs J. Howard, Tathwell, Louth.
Dr S. J. S. Hughes, Weedon Bec, Northampton.
Harold Jackson, Louth
J. A. Johnston, Lincoln.
Mr and Mrs A. King, North Somercotes, Louth
Miss Dorothy King, Spilsby.
Mrs B. Kirkham, Hogsthorpe, Skegness.

Terence R. Leach, Dunholme, Lincoln.
Leicester University Library, Leicester.
Mrs J. Mostyn Lewis, Claxby, Market Rasen
Lincolnshire Library Service, Lincoln (eleven copies).
Nick Lyons, Saxby All Saints, Brigg.
Mr H. Macallister, Wissett, Halesworth.
Mrs Jane Madden, Thorpe St Andrew, Norwich (two copies).
Dr Peter Mangold, London.
Jean Martin, Kenilworth.
N. J. A. Martin, Wirral (two copies)
T. J. Martin, Dorridge, Solihull.
Miss L. E. Matthews, Reydon, Southwold.
Suzanne Mendel, Utterby Louth.
Michael Millgate, Toronto, Ontario.
Mrs Pauline M. Moore, Woodbridge.
D. C. Mordaunt, Cleethorpes.
Mrs G. Mouser, Weeley Heath, Clacton on Sea.
Miss F. A. R. Murray, Lincoln.
J. Murray, Tealby.
Oglethorpe University, Charles Weltner Library, Atlanta, Georgia.
Dr R. J. Olney, Peckham Rye, London.
Mrs L. Ormond, King's College, London.
Patrick O'Shaughnessy, Boston.
Richard Osmond, Oxford.
Dr D. M. Owen, Thimbleby, Horncastle.
Dr Robert Pacey, Burgh Le Marsh, Skegness.
Norman Page, Oakham, Rutland.
Roger Peattie, University of Calgary, Alberta.
Bob Porter, Preston, Lancashire.
A. J. Pothecary, Alconbury, Huntingdon.
Dinah Purton, Coltishall, Norwich.
Dr Charles Rawding, Market Rasen.
Christopher Ricks, Lasborough Park, Tetbury.
Philip Riley, Uppingham, Rutland.
Mrs J. Robb, Oxshott, Surrey.
Mr and Mrs R. Pettit, Chapel St Leonard's, Lincolnshire.
Mr D. N. Robinson, Louth.
Royal Holloway and Bedford New College Library, Egham, Surrey.
T. W. Royce, Spalding.
St Mary's School, Colchester, Essex.
Dr Rosemary Scott, Rochester, Kent.
Edgar F. Shannon, Jr., University of Virginia, Charlottesville.
K. W. Sidebotham, Louth.
Dr Roger Simpson, University of East Anglia, Norwich.

Mrs Madelaine Anne Smith, Peterborough.
Mr Utterby Snaith, Spalding.
Christine Spreadbury, Cropston, Leicester.
Mrs Gillian Stafford, Tealby (two copies).
Stanilands (Booksellers), Stamford.
Mr A. K. Templeton, Bangor, Co. Down.
Mrs Mary Tennyson d'Eyncourt, Gijon, Spain (three copies).
Texas Christian University, Mary Couts Burnett Library, Fort Worth, Texas.
Ann Thwaite, Low Tharston, Norfolk.
Mrs J. Toyne, Lincoln.
Mrs Jean E. Tyas, Guisborough, Cleveland.
Mrs E. D. Underwood, Louth.
Mr Richard Underwood, Hove, Sussex.
Mrs Joan Varley, Lincoln.
Mrs F. A. Wale, Torrington, Devon.
Michael Weaver, Woodbridge, Suffolk.
Dr I. M. Webb, Willingdon, Eastbourne.
Anne Wilkins, Stamford.
Mrs Elsbeth Williams, Newcastle upon Tyne.
Mrs E. D. Williams, Stoke Holy Cross, Norwich.
Miss J. Williams, Hereford.
Woodbridge School, Woodbridge, Suffolk.